T0311542

Knitted Christmas Stockings

25 festive designs to make for family and friends

Knitted Christmas Stockings

25 festive designs to make
for family and friends

Emilee Reynolds

THE GUILD OF MASTER CRAFTSMAN PUBLICATIONS

Contents

Introduction

Do you ever find yourself hoping that Christmas would last a little longer each year? I don't mean the hustle and bustle but the serenity of the season. Well, in my little world, Christmas is pretty much year-round. I design and knit Christmas stockings. I can't explain the feeling when a stocking has been knitted from start to finish but it brings me joy and a sense of accomplishment.

I learned how to knit in 2004 when I asked my grandma to teach me. I wanted to continue a family tradition that has been around since 1959. That year, my great-grandma, Elizabeth Barton Grant, surprised her children, their spouses and their children with a personalized knitted Christmas stocking. Later, my grandma, Carol Grant, took over the tradition. When I was first married, I wanted to keep the tradition alive and knew my grandma wasn't going to be around much longer. So, a Christmas stocking was my first knit project.

Some might start by knitting a washcloth or a scarf to get the hang of it but I didn't want to waste any time. I had a purpose. However, there weren't a ton of stocking pattern books and I wanted a variety of designs. At that time, I believe I was watching quite a lot of *Project Runway*. I do not sew but was inspired to focus on cohesive collections and create themes. Fast forward to last year, I decided to help a little by giving families in need brand new Christmas stockings from 52 newly designed patterns. I've since continued that tradition as well as the family tradition.

In this book, you will find 25 fun-loving Christmas stocking designs, featuring everything from elves to nativity scene characters. Each stocking is created through one main pattern (the way grandma taught). The projects have colour charts as well as written instructions to make it easy to follow the patterns. The stockings range from Beginner (1 star) to Advanced (3 stars). There is also a list of tools, materials and techniques to explain knitting basics, and ideas to personalize your stockings. I truly hope you enjoy these unique and innovative designs.

Modern Designs

Christmas Star

Skill level

Materials
- Pair of 3.5mm (US4) knitting needles
- 3.5mm (US4) double-pointed knitting needles
- Loops & Threads Impeccable Solid Yarn,
  100% acrylic (285yd/260m per 127.5g ball):
  1 x 127.5g ball in Gold, White, Soft Rose
- Tapestry needle
- 2 stitch holders
- Jingle bell (optional)

Finished size
22in (56cm) long and 6½in (16.5cm) wide

Starting the stocking
Cast on 60 sts in Gold.
Cuff
Working in k2, p2 rib, continue for 7 rows. Break yarn, leaving about 10in (25cm) for sewing up.

Personalize your stocking
If you would like a name or date on your stocking, use the alphabet and number chart provided on page 138, and a yarn colour of your choice (shown in Gold).
Row 1: P 1 row in White.
Row 2: K 1 row and inc 1 st at end of row (61 sts).
Rows 3–9: Continue to p 1 row and k 1 row in White for 7 more rows for a total of 9 rows.

Main design

Row 10: Using st st, follow the chart opposite in Gold.

Dec 1st each side on rows 39, 49, 59 and 69 (53 sts).

Work to end of chart, end on a p row.

Be sure to cross yarns when changing colours to avoid leaving a hole in the work.

Break yarn, leaving an 18in (46cm) end for sewing up.

With RS facing you, sl first 13 sts onto a stitch holder for right half of heel; sl next 27 sts onto a stitch holder for instep; sl last 13 sts onto a dpn for left half of heel.

Left half of heel

With WS facing you, k and p the following rows in Soft Rose.

First row: P.

Next row: Sl 1, k12.

Repeat these two rows for a total of 8 times (18 rows on heel).

Turn heel as follows:

Row 1: P2, p2tog, p1, turn.
Row 2: Sl 1, k3, turn.
Row 3: P3, p2tog, p1, turn.
Row 4: Sl 1, k4, turn.
Row 5: P4, p2tog, p1, turn.
Row 6: Sl 1, k5, turn.
Row 7: P5, p2tog, p1, turn.
Row 8: Sl 1, k6, turn.
Row 9: P6, p2tog, p1 (8 sts).

Break yarn, place sts on stitch holder or leave on needle.

Right half of heel

With RS facing you, k and p the following rows in Soft Rose.

First row: K.

Next row: Sl 1, p12.

Repeat these two rows for a total of 8 times (18 rows on heel).

Turn heel as follows:

Row 1: K2, SKP, k1, turn.
Row 2: Sl 1, p3, turn.
Row 3: K3, SKP, k1, turn.
Row 4: Sl 1, p4, turn.
Row 5: K4, SKP, k1, turn.
Row 6: Sl 1, p5, turn.
Row 7: K5, SKP, k1, turn.

Row 8: Sl 1, p6, turn.
Row 9: K6, SKP, k1 (8 sts).
Break yarn.

Next: Rejoin yarn, k across 8 sts starting on the outer edge of the RS; pick up and k 9 sts on inner edge of half heel; k across 27 sts of instep; pick up and k 9 sts on inner edge of other half heel; k across 8 sts (61 sts).
P 1 row.

Gusset and instep

Row 1: K14, k2tog, k29, SKP, k14 (59 sts).
Row 2: P.
Row 3: K13, k2tog, k29, SKP, k13 (57 sts).
Row 4: P.
Row 5: K12, k2tog, k29, SKP, k12 (55 sts).
Row 6: P.
Row 7: K11, k2tog, k29, SKP, k11 (53 sts).
Row 8: P.
Row 9: K10, k2tog, k29, SKP, k10 (51 sts).
Row 10: P.
Row 11: K9, k2tog, k29, SKP, k9 (49 sts).
Row 12: P.
K 1 row, p 1 row for 22 rows in White.
Row 23 (decrease row): K23, k2tog, k24 (48 sts).
Row 24: P.
Break yarn, leaving a 14in (36cm) end for sewing up.

Shape toe

Row 1: Using Gold, k9, k2tog, k2, SKP, k18, k2tog, k2, SKP, k9 (44 sts).
Row 2: P.
Row 3: K8, k2tog, k2, SKP, k16, k2tog, k2, SKP, k8 (40 sts).
Row 4: P.
Row 5: K7, k2tog, k2, SKP, k14, k2tog, k2, SKP, k7 (36 sts).
Row 6: P.
Row 7: K6, k2tog, k2, SKP, k12, k2tog, k2, SKP, k6 (32 sts).
Row 8: P.
Row 9: K5, k2tog, k2, SKP, k10, k2tog,

k2, SKP, k5 (28 sts).
Row 10: P.
Row 11: K4, k2tog, k2, SKP, k8, k2tog, k2, SKP, k4 (24 sts).
Row 12: P.
Row 13: K3, k2tog, k2, SKP, k6, k2tog, k2, SKP, k3 (20 sts).
Row 14: P.
Row 15: K2, k2tog, k2, SKP, k4, k2tog, k2, SKP, k2 (16 sts).
After last row, with WS facing you, place first 4 sts on a dpn. Sl next 8 sts to a second needle and sl last 4 sts to third needle.
Begin with fourth st, sl 4 sts from first needle, k last 4 sts from third needle to same needle with edges at the centre of needle. Needles should be parallel with one another.
Break yarn, leaving a 14in (36cm) length for weaving the toe.

Weaving toe

Thread end of yarn into tapestry needle and weave sts together as follows:

Front needle: Pass needle through as if to k and sl st off, pass through second st of front needle as if to p but leave st on needle, draw yarn through.

Back needle: Pass needle through as if to p and sl st off, pass through second st of back needle as if to k but leave st on needle, draw yarn through.
Repeat until all sts are joined.
Fasten off.

Completing the stocking

Use a tapestry needle to sew in all ends securely. Weave in all ends using matching colours. Use a mattress stitch to join the seams. Sew the jingle bell onto the toe. To make a chain, use a dpn and cast on 3 sts. K each row until you have the desired length for your chain. Use a tapestry needle to sew the chain onto the top of the stocking.

Christmas Star chart
Each square on the chart represents one stitch.

Key:
☐ White   ▨ Gold

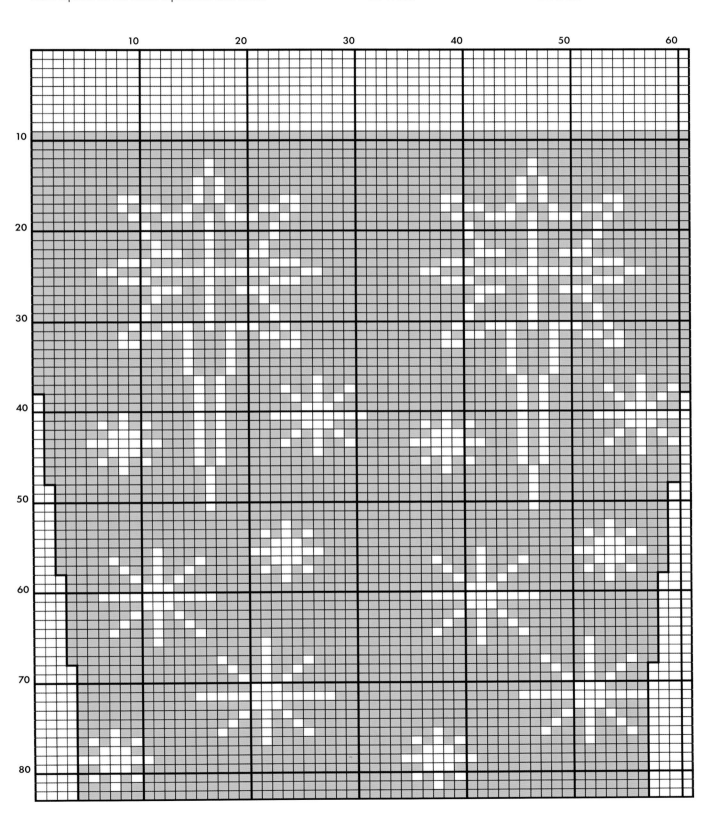

Snow Shapes

Skill level

Materials
- Pair of 3.5mm (US4) knitting needles
- 3.5mm (US4) double-pointed knitting needles
- Loops & Threads Impeccable Solid Yarn, 100% acrylic (285yd/260m per 127.5g ball): 1 x 127.5g ball in Thunder, Gold, White
- Tapestry needle
- 2 stitch holders
- Jingle bell (optional)

Finished size
22in (56cm) long and 6½in (16.5cm) wide

Starting the stocking
Cast on 60 sts in Thunder.
Cuff
Working in k2, p2 rib, continue for 7 rows. Break yarn, leaving about 10in (25cm) for sewing up.

Personalize your stocking
If you would like a name or date on your stocking, use the alphabet and number chart provided on page 138, and a yarn colour of your choice (shown in Gold).
Row 1: P 1 row in White.
Row 2: K 1 row and inc 1 st at end of row (61 sts).
Rows 3–9: Continue to p 1 row and k 1 row in White for 7 more rows for a total of 9 rows.

Main design

Row 10: Using st st, follow the chart opposite in Thunder.

Dec 1st each side on rows 39, 49, 59 and 69 (53 sts).

Work to end of chart, end on a p row. Be sure to cross yarns when changing colours to avoid leaving a hole in the work.

Break yarn, leaving an 18in (46cm) end for sewing up.

With RS facing you, sl first 13 sts onto a stitch holder for right half of heel; sl next 27 sts onto a stitch holder for instep; sl last 13 sts onto a dpn for left half of heel.

Left half of heel

With WS facing you, k and p the following rows in Gold.

First row: P.

Next row: Sl 1, k12.

Repeat these two rows for a total of 8 times (18 rows on heel).

Turn heel as follows:

Row 1: P2, p2tog, p1, turn.
Row 2: Sl 1, k3, turn.
Row 3: P3, p2tog, p1, turn.
Row 4: Sl 1, k4, turn.
Row 5: P4, p2tog, p1, turn.
Row 6: Sl 1, k5, turn.
Row 7: P5, p2tog, p1, turn.
Row 8: Sl 1, k6, turn.
Row 9: P6, p2tog, p1 (8 sts).
Break yarn, place sts on stitch holder or leave on needle.

Right half of heel

With RS facing you, k and p the following rows in Gold.

First row: K.

Next row: Sl 1, p12.

Repeat these two rows for a total of 8 times (18 rows on heel).

Turn heel as follows:

Row 1: K2, SKP, k1, turn.
Row 2: Sl 1, p3, turn.
Row 3: K3, SKP, k1, turn.
Row 4: Sl 1, p4, turn.
Row 5: K4, SKP, k1, turn.
Row 6: Sl 1, p5, turn.
Row 7: K5, SKP, k1, turn.

Row 8: Sl 1, p6, turn.
Row 9: K6, SKP, k1 (8 sts).
Break yarn.
Next: Rejoin yarn, k across 8 sts starting on the outer edge of the RS; pick up and k 9 sts on inner edge of half heel; k across 27 sts of instep; pick up and k 9 sts on inner edge of other half heel; k across 8 sts (61 sts).
P 1 row.

Gusset and instep

Row 1: K14, k2tog, k29, SKP, k14 (59 sts).
Row 2: P.
Row 3: K13, k2tog, k29, SKP, k13 (57 sts).
Row 4: P.
Row 5: K12, k2tog, k29, SKP, k12 (55 sts).
Row 6: P.
Row 7: K11, k2tog, k29, SKP, k11 (53 sts).
Row 8: P.
Row 9: K10, k2tog, k29, SKP, k10 (51 sts).
Row 10: P.
Row 11: K9, k2tog, k29, SKP, k9 (49 sts).
Row 12: P.
K 1 row, p 1 row for 22 rows in White.
Row 23 (decrease row): K23, k2tog, k24 (48 sts).
Row 24: P.
Break yarn, leaving a 14in (36cm) end for sewing up.

Shape toe

Row 1: Using Thunder, k9, k2tog, k2, SKP, k18, k2tog, k2, SKP, k9 (44 sts).
Row 2: P.
Row 3: K8, k2tog, k2, SKP, k16, k2tog, k2, SKP, k8 (40 sts).
Row 4: P.
Row 5: K7, k2tog, k2, SKP, k14, k2tog, k2, SKP, k7 (36 sts).
Row 6: P.
Row 7: K6, k2tog, k2, SKP, k12, k2tog, k2, SKP, k6 (32 sts).
Row 8: P.
Row 9: K5, k2tog, k2, SKP, k10, k2tog,

k2, SKP, k5 (28 sts).
Row 10: P.
Row 11: K4, k2tog, k2, SKP, k8, k2tog, k2, SKP, k4 (24 sts).
Row 12: P.
Row 13: K3, k2tog, k2, SKP, k6, k2tog, k2, SKP, k3 (20 sts).
Row 14: P.
Row 15: K2, k2tog, k2, SKP, k4, k2tog, k2, SKP, k2 (16 sts).

After last row, with WS facing you, place first 4 sts on a dpn. Sl next 8 sts to a second needle and sl last 4 sts to a third needle.

Begin with fourth st, sl 4 sts from first needle, k last 4 sts from third needle to same needle with edges at the centre of needle. Needles should be parallel with one another.

Break yarn, leaving a 14in (36cm) length for weaving the toe.

Weaving toe

Thread end of yarn into tapestry needle and weave sts together as follows:

Front needle: Pass needle through as if to k and sl st off, pass through second st of front needle as if to p but leave st on needle, draw yarn through.

Back needle: Pass needle through as if to p and sl st off, pass through second st of back needle as if to k but leave st on needle, draw yarn through.

Repeat until all sts are joined.

Fasten off.

Completing the stocking

Use a tapestry needle to sew in all ends securely. Weave in all ends using matching colours. Use a mattress stitch to join the seams. Sew the jingle bell onto the toe. To make a chain, use a dpn and cast on 3 sts. K each row until you have the desired length for your chain. Use a tapestry needle to sew the chain onto the top of the stocking.

Snow Shapes chart

Each square on the chart represents one stitch.

Key:
Thunder   White

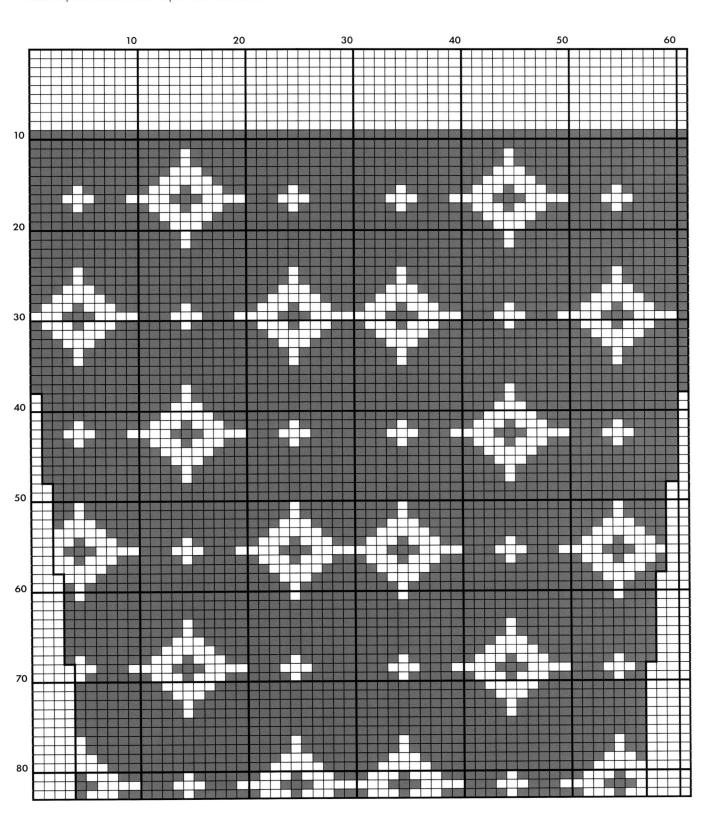

Starry Night

Skill level

Materials
- Pair of 3.5mm (US4) knitting needles
- 3.5mm (US4) double-pointed knitting needles
- Loops & Threads Impeccable Solid Yarn, 100% acrylic (285yd/260m per 127.5g ball): 1 x 127.5g ball in Pale Grey, White, Thunder
- Oddment of Gold
- Tapestry needle
- 2 stitch holders
- Jingle bell (optional)

Finished size
22in (56cm) long and 6½in (16.5cm) wide

Starting the stocking
Cast on 60 sts in Pale Grey.
Cuff
Working in k2, p2 rib, continue for 7 rows. Break yarn, leaving about 10in (25cm) for sewing up.

Personalize your stocking
If you would like a name or date on your stocking, use the alphabet and number chart provided on page 138, and a yarn colour of your choice (shown in Gold).
Row 1: P 1 row in White.
Row 2: K 1 row and inc 1 st at end of row (61 sts).
Rows 3–9: Continue to p 1 row and k 1 row in White for 7 more rows for a total of 9 rows.

Main design

Row 10: Using st st, follow the chart opposite in Pale Grey.

Dec 1 st each side on rows 39, 49, 59 and 69 (53 sts).

Work to end of chart, end on a p row. Be sure to cross yarns when changing colours to avoid leaving a hole in the work.

Break yarn, leaving an 18in (46cm) end for sewing up.

With RS facing you, sl first 13 sts onto a stitch holder for right half of heel; sl next 27 sts onto a stitch holder for instep; sl last 13 sts onto a dpn for left half of heel.

Left half of heel

With WS facing you, k and p the following rows in Thunder.

First row: P.

Next row: Sl 1, k12.

Repeat these two rows for a total of 8 times (18 rows on heel).

Turn heel as follows:

Row 1: P2, p2tog, p1, turn.
Row 2: Sl 1, k3, turn.
Row 3: P3, p2tog, p1, turn.
Row 4: Sl 1, k4, turn.
Row 5: P4, p2tog, p1, turn.
Row 6: Sl 1, k5, turn.
Row 7: P5, p2tog, p1, turn.
Row 8: Sl 1, k6, turn.
Row 9: P6, p2tog, p1 (8 sts).

Break yarn, place sts on stitch holder or leave on needle.

Right half of heel

With RS facing you, k and p the following rows in Thunder.

First row: K.

Next row: Sl 1, p12.

Repeat these two rows for a total of 8 times (18 rows on heel).

Turn heel as follows:

Row 1: K2, SKP, k1, turn.
Row 2: Sl 1, p3, turn.
Row 3: K3, SKP, k1, turn.
Row 4: Sl 1, p4, turn.
Row 5: K4, SKP, k1, turn.
Row 6: Sl 1, p5, turn.
Row 7: K5, SKP, k1, turn.
Row 8: Sl 1, p6, turn.
Row 9: K6, SKP, k1 (8 sts).

Break yarn.

Next: Rejoin yarn, k across 8 sts starting on the outer edge of the RS; pick up and k 9 sts on inner edge of half heel; k across 27 sts of instep; pick up and k 9 sts on inner edge of other half heel; k across 8 sts (61 sts).

P 1 row.

Gusset and instep

Row 1: K14, k2tog, k29, SKP, k14 (59 sts).
Row 2: P.
Row 3: K13, k2tog, k29, SKP, k13 (57 sts).
Row 4: P.
Row 5: K12, k2tog, k29, SKP, k12 (55 sts).
Row 6: P.
Row 7: K11, k2tog, k29, SKP, k11 (53 sts).
Row 8: P.
Row 9: K10, k2tog, k29, SKP, k10 (51 sts).
Row 10: P.
Row 11: K9, k2tog, k29, SKP, k9 (49 sts).
Row 12: P.

K 1 row, p 1 row for 22 rows in White.

Row 23 (decrease row): K23, k2tog, k24 (48 sts).
Row 24: P.

Break yarn, leaving a 14in (36cm) end for sewing up.

Shape toe

Row 1: Using Pale Grey, k9, k2tog, k2, SKP, k18, k2tog, k2, SKP, k9 (44 sts).
Row 2: P.
Row 3: K8, k2tog, k2, SKP, k16, k2tog, k2, SKP, k8 (40 sts).
Row 4: P.
Row 5: K7, k2tog, k2, SKP, k14, k2tog, k2, SKP, k7 (36 sts).
Row 6: P.
Row 7: K6, k2tog, k2, SKP, k12, k2tog, k2, SKP, k6 (32 sts).
Row 8: P.

Row 9: K5, k2tog, k2, SKP, k10, k2tog, k2, SKP, k5 (28 sts).
Row 10: P.
Row 11: K4, k2tog, k2, SKP, k8, k2tog, k2, SKP, k4 (24 sts).
Row 12: P.
Row 13: K3, k2tog, k2, SKP, k6, k2tog, k2, SKP, k3 (20 sts).
Row 14: P.
Row 15: K2, k2tog, k2, SKP, k4, k2tog, k2, SKP, k2 (16 sts).

After last row, with WS facing you, place first 4 sts on a dpn. Sl next 8 sts to a second needle and sl last 4 sts to third needle.

Begin with fourth st, sl 4 sts from first needle, k last 4 sts from third needle to same needle with edges at the centre of needle. Needles should be parallel with one another.

Break yarn, leaving a 14in (36cm) length for weaving the toe.

Weaving the toe

Thread end of yarn into tapestry needle and weave sts together as follows:

Front needle: Pass needle through as if to k and sl st off, pass through second st of front needle as if to p but leave st on needle, draw yarn through.

Back needle: Pass needle through as if to p and sl st off, pass through second st of back needle as if to k but leave st on needle, draw yarn through.

Repeat until all sts are joined.

Fasten off.

Completing the stocking

Use a tapestry needle to sew in all ends securely. Weave in all ends using matching colours. Use a mattress stitch to join the seams. Sew the jingle bell onto the toe. To make a chain, use a dpn and cast on 3 sts. K each row until you have the desired length for your chain. Use a tapestry needle to sew the chain onto the top of the stocking.

Starry Night chart

Each square on the chart represents one stitch.

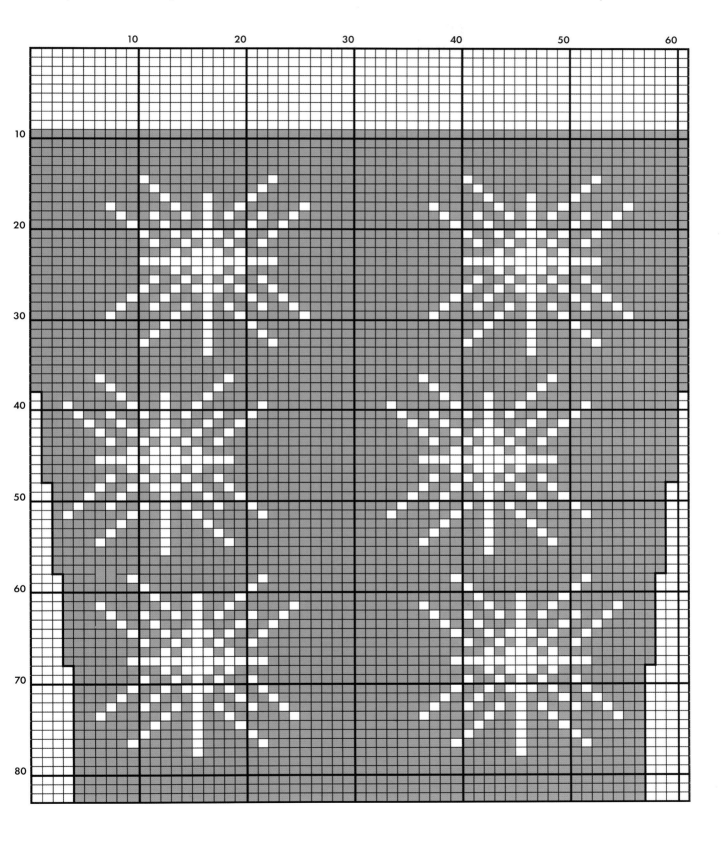

Soft and Cosy

Skill level

Materials
- Pair of 3.5mm (US4) knitting needles
- 3.5mm (US4) double-pointed knitting needles
- Loops & Threads Impeccable Solid Yarn, 100% acrylic (285yd/260m per 127.5g ball): 1 x 127.5g ball in Soft Rose, White, Gold
- Tapestry needle
- 2 stitch holders
- Jingle bell (optional)

Finished size
22in (56cm) long and 6½in (16.5cm) wide

Starting the stocking
Cast on 60 sts in Soft Rose.
Cuff
Working in k2, p2 rib, continue for 7 rows. Break yarn, leaving about 10in (25cm) for sewing up.

Personalize your stocking
If you would like a name or date on your stocking, use the alphabet and number chart provided on page 138, and a yarn colour of your choice (shown in Gold).
Row 1: P 1 row in White.
Row 2: K 1 row and inc 1 st at end of row (61 sts).
Rows 3–9: Continue to p 1 row and k 1 row in White for 7 more rows for a total of 9 rows.

Main design

Row 10: Using st st, follow the chart opposite in Soft Rose.

Dec 1 st each side on rows 39, 49, 59 and 69 (53 sts).

Work to end of chart, end on a p row. Be sure to cross yarns when changing colours to avoid leaving a hole in the work.

Break yarn, leaving an 18in (46cm) end for sewing up.

With RS facing you, sl first 13 sts onto a stitch holder for right half of heel; sl next 27 sts onto a stitch holder for instep; sl last 13 sts onto a dpn for left half of heel.

Left half of heel

With WS facing you, k and p the following rows in Gold.

First row: P.

Next row: Sl 1, k12.

Repeat these two rows for a total of 8 times (18 rows on heel).

Turn heel as follows:

Row 1: P2, p2tog, p1, turn.

Row 2: Sl 1, k3, turn.

Row 3: P3, p2tog, p1, turn.

Row 4: Sl 1, k4, turn.

Row 5: P4, p2tog, p1, turn.

Row 6: Sl 1, k5, turn.

Row 7: P5, p2tog, p1, turn.

Row 8: Sl 1, k6, turn.

Row 9: P6, p2tog, p1 (8 sts).

Break yarn, place sts on stitch holder or leave on needle.

Right half of heel

With RS facing you, k and p the following rows in Gold.

First row: K.

Next row: Sl 1, p12.

Repeat these two rows for a total of 8 times (18 rows on heel.)

Turn heel as follows:

Row 1: K2, SKP, k1, turn.

Row 2: Sl 1, p3, turn.

Row 3: K3, SKP, k1, turn.

Row 4: Sl 1, p4, turn.

Row 5: K4, SKP, k1, turn.

Row 6: Sl 1, p5, turn.

Row 7: K5, SKP, k1, turn.

Row 8: Sl 1, p6, turn.

Row 9: K6, SKP, k1 (8 sts).

Break yarn.

Next: Rejoin yarn, k across 8 sts starting on the outer edge of the RS; pick up and k 9 sts on inner edge of half heel; k across 27 sts of instep; pick up and k 9 sts on inner edge of other half heel; k across 8 sts (61 sts).

P 1 row.

Gusset and instep

Row 1: K14, k2tog, k29, SKP, k14 (59 sts).

Row 2: P.

Row 3: K13, k2tog, k29, SKP, k13 (57 sts).

Row 4: P.

Row 5: K12, k2tog, k29, SKP, k12 (55 sts).

Row 6: P.

Row 7: K11, k2tog, k29, SKP, k11 (53 sts).

Row 8: P.

Row 9: K10, k2tog, k29, SKP, k10 (51 sts).

Row 10: P.

Row 11: K9, k2tog, k29, SKP, k9 (49 sts).

Row 12: P.

K 1 row, p 1 row for 22 rows in White.

Row 23 (decrease row): K23, k2tog, k24 (48 sts).

Row 24: P.

Break yarn, leaving a 14in (36cm) end for sewing up.

Shape toe

Row 1: Using Soft Rose, k9, k2tog, k2, SKP, k18, k2tog, k2, SKP, k9 (44 sts).

Row 2: P.

Row 3: K8, k2tog, k2, SKP, k16, k2tog, k2, SKP, k8 (40 sts).

Row 4: P.

Row 5: K7, k2tog, k2, SKP, k14, k2tog, k2, SKP, k7 (36 sts).

Row 6: P.

Row 7: K6, k2tog, k2, SKP, k12, k2tog, k2, SKP, k6 (32 sts).

Row 8: P.

Row 9: K5, k2tog, k2, SKP, k10, k2tog, k2, SKP, k5 (28 sts).

Row 10: P.

Row 11: K4, k2tog, k2, SKP, k8, k2tog, k2, SKP, k4 (24 sts).

Row 12: P.

Row 13: K3, k2tog, k2, SKP, k6, k2tog, k2, SKP, k3 (20 sts).

Row 14: P.

Row 15: K2, k2tog, k2, SKP, k4, k2tog, k2, SKP, k2 (16 sts).

After last row, with WS facing you, place first 4 sts on a dpn. Sl next 8 sts to a second needle and sl last 4 sts to third needle.

Begin with fourth st, sl 4 sts from first needle, k last 4 sts from third needle to same needle with edges at the centre of needle. Needles should be parallel with one another.

Break yarn, leaving a 14in (36cm) length for weaving the toe.

Weaving the toe

Thread end of yarn into tapestry needle and weave sts together as follows:

Front needle: Pass needle through as if to k and sl st off, pass through second st of front needle as if to p but leave st on needle, draw yarn through.

Back needle: Pass needle through as if to p and sl st off, pass through second st of back needle as if to k but leave st on needle, draw yarn through.

Repeat until all sts are joined.

Fasten off.

Completing the stocking

Use a tapestry needle to sew in all ends securely. Weave in all ends using matching colours. Use a mattress stitch to join the seams. Sew the jingle bell onto the toe. To make a chain, use a dpn and cast on 3 sts. K each row until you have the desired length for your chain. Use a tapestry needle to sew the chain onto the top of the stocking.

Soft and Cosy chart

Each square on the chart represents one stitch.

Key:

☐ White   ☐ Soft Rose

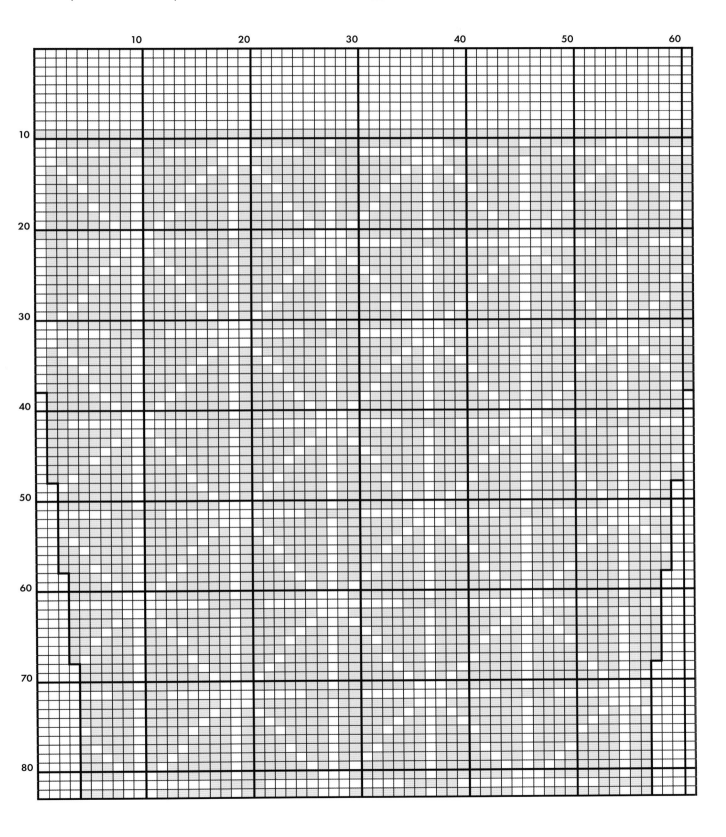

Stylish Squares

Skill level

Materials
- Pair of 3.5mm (US4) knitting needles
- 3.5mm (US4) double-pointed knitting needles
- Loops & Threads Impeccable Solid Yarn, 100% acrylic (285yd/260m per 127.5g ball): 1 x 127.5g ball in Pale Grey, White, Black
- Oddment of Gold
- Tapestry needle
- 2 stitch holders
- Jingle bell (optional)

Finished size
22in (56cm) long and 6½in (16.5cm) wide

Starting the stocking
Cast on 60 sts in Black.
Cuff
Working in k2, p2 rib, continue for 7 rows. Break yarn, leaving about 10in (25cm) for sewing up.

Personalize your stocking
If you would like a name or date on your stocking, use the alphabet and number chart provided on page 138, and a yarn colour of your choice (shown in Gold).
Row 1: P 1 row in White.
Row 2: K 1 row and inc 1 st at end of row (61 sts).
Rows 3–9: Continue to p 1 row and k 1 row in White for 7 more rows for a total of 9 rows.

Main design

Row 10: Using st st, follow the chart opposite in Black.

Dec 1 st each side on rows 39, 49, 59 and 69 (53 sts).

Work to end of chart, end on a p row. Be sure to cross yarns when changing colours to avoid leaving a hole in the work.

Break yarn, leaving an 18in (46cm) end for sewing up.

With RS facing you, sl first 13 sts onto a stitch holder for right half of heel; sl next 27 sts onto a stitch holder for instep; sl last 13 sts onto a dpn for left half of heel.

Left half of heel

With WS facing you, k and p the following rows in Pale Grey.

First row: P.

Next row: Sl 1, k12.

Repeat these two rows for a total of 8 times (18 rows on heel).

Turn heel as follows:

Row 1: P2, p2tog, p1, turn.

Row 2: Sl 1, k3, turn.

Row 3: P3, p2tog, p1, turn.

Row 4: Sl 1, k4, turn.

Row 5: P4, p2tog, p1, turn.

Row 6: Sl 1, k5, turn.

Row 7: P5, p2tog, p1, turn.

Row 8: Sl 1, k6, turn.

Row 9: P6, p2tog, p1 (8 sts).

Break yarn, place sts on stitch holder or leave on needle.

Right half of heel

With RS facing you, k and p the following rows in Pale Grey.

First row: K.

Next row: Sl 1, p12.

Repeat these two rows for a total of 8 times (18 rows on heel).

Turn heel as follows:

Row 1: K2, SKP, k1, turn.

Row 2: Sl 1, p3, turn.

Row 3: K3, SKP, k1, turn.

Row 4: Sl 1, p4, turn.

Row 5: K4, SKP, k1, turn.

Row 6: Sl 1, p5, turn.

Row 7: K5, SKP, k1, turn.

Row 8: Sl 1, p6, turn.

Row 9: K6, SKP, k1 (8 sts).

Break yarn.

Next: Rejoin yarn, k across 8 sts starting on the outer edge of the RS; pick up and k 9 sts on inner edge of half heel; k across 27 sts of instep; pick up and k 9 sts on inner edge of other half heel; k across 8 sts (61 sts).

P 1 row.

Gusset and instep

Row 1: K14, k2tog, k29, SKP, k14 (59 sts).

Row 2: P.

Row 3: K13, k2tog, k29, SKP, k13 (57 sts).

Row 4: P.

Row 5: K12, k2tog, k29, SKP, k12 (55 sts).

Row 6: P.

Row 7: K11, k2tog, k29, SKP, k11 (53 sts).

Row 8: P.

Row 9: K10, k2tog, k29, SKP, k10 (51 sts).

Row 10: P.

Row 11: K9, k2tog, k29, SKP, k9 (49 sts).

Row 12: P.

K 1 row, p 1 row for 22 rows in White.

Row 23 (decrease row): K23, k2tog, k24 (48 sts).

Row 24: P.

Break yarn, leaving a 14in (36cm) end for sewing up.

Shape toe

Row 1: Using Black, k9, k2tog, k2, SKP, k18, k2tog, k2, SKP, k9 (44 sts).

Row 2: P.

Row 3: K8, k2tog, k2, SKP, k16, k2tog, k2, SKP, k8 (40 sts).

Row 4: P.

Row 5: K7, k2tog, k2, SKP, k14, k2tog, k2, SKP, k7 (36 sts).

Row 6: P.

Row 7: K6, k2tog, k2, SKP, k12, k2tog, k2, SKP, k6 (32 sts).

Row 8: P.

Row 9: K5, k2tog, k2, SKP, k10, k2tog, k2, SKP, k5 (28 sts).

Row 10: P.

Row 11: K4, k2tog, k2, SKP, k8, k2tog, k2, SKP, k4 (24 sts).

Row 12: P.

Row 13: K3, k2tog, k2, SKP, k6, k2tog, k2, SKP, k3 (20 sts).

Row 14: P.

Row 15: K2, k2tog, k2, SKP, k4, k2tog, k2, SKP, k2 (16 sts).

After last row, with WS facing you, place first 4 sts on a dpn. Sl next 8 sts to a second needle and sl last 4 sts to third needle.

Begin with fourth st, sl 4 sts from first needle, k last 4 sts from third needle to same needle with edges at the centre of needle. Needles should be parallel with one another.

Break yarn, leaving a 14in (36cm) length for weaving the toe.

Weaving the toe

Thread end of yarn into tapestry needle and weave sts together as follows:

Front needle: Pass needle through as if to k and sl st off, pass through second st of front needle as if to p but leave st on needle, draw yarn through.

Back needle: Pass needle through as if to p and sl st off, pass through second st of back needle as if to k but leave st on needle, draw yarn through.

Repeat until all sts are joined.

Fasten off.

Completing the stocking

Use a tapestry needle to sew in all ends securely. Weave in all ends using matching colours. Use a mattress stitch to join the seams. Sew the jingle bell onto the toe. To make a chain, use a dpn and cast on 3 sts. K each row until you have the desired length for your chain. Use a tapestry needle to sew the chain onto the top of the stocking.

Stylish Squares chart

Each square on the chart represents one stitch.

Key:
■ Black   ☐ White

Christmas
Elves

Papa

Skill level

Materials
- Pair of 3.5mm (US4) knitting needles
- 3.5mm (US4) double-pointed knitting needles
- Red Heart Super Saver, 100% acrylic (364yd/333m per 198g ball):
  1 x 198g ball in Cherry Red, Paddy Green, Black, Aran
- Oddments of Petal Pink, Grey Heather
- Bernat Pipsqueak, 100% polyester (101yd/92m per 100g ball):
  1 x 100g ball in Whitey White
- Tapestry needle
- 2 stitch holders
- Jingle bell (optional)

Finished size
22in (56cm) long and 6½in (16.5cm) wide

Starting the stocking
Cast on 60 sts in Cherry Red.
Cuff
Working in k2, p2 rib, continue for 7 rows. Break yarn, leaving about 10in (25cm) for sewing up.

Personalize your stocking
If you would like a name or date on your stocking, use the alphabet and number chart provided on page 138, and a yarn colour of your choice.
Row 1: P 1 row in Aran.
Row 2: K 1 row and inc 1 st at end of row (61 sts).
Rows 3–9: Continue to p 1 row and k 1 row in Aran for 7 more rows for a total of 9 rows.

Main design
Row 10: Using st st, follow the chart opposite in Paddy Green.

Dec 1 st each side on rows 39, 49, 59 and 69 (53 sts).

Work to end of chart, end on a p row. Be sure to cross yarns when changing colours to avoid leaving a hole in the work.

Break yarn, leaving an 18in (46cm) end for sewing up.

With RS facing you, sl first 13 sts onto a stitch holder for right half of heel; sl next 27 sts onto a stitch holder for instep; sl last 13 sts onto a dpn for left half of heel.

Left half of heel
With WS facing you, k and p the following rows in Cherry Red.

First row: P.

Next row: Sl 1, k12.

Repeat these two rows for a total of 8 times (18 rows on heel).

Turn heel as follows:

Row 1: P2, p2tog, p1, turn.

Row 2: Sl 1, k3, turn.

Row 3: P3, p2tog, p1, turn.

Row 4: Sl 1, k4, turn.

Row 5: P4, p2tog, p1, turn.

Row 6: Sl 1, k5, turn.

Row 7: P5, p2tog, p1, turn.

Row 8: Sl 1, k6, turn.

Row 9: P6, p2tog, p1 (8 sts).

Break yarn, place sts on stitch holder or leave on needle.

Right half of heel
With RS facing you, k and p the following rows in Cherry Red.

First row: K.

Next row: Sl 1, p12.

Repeat these two rows for a total of 8 times (18 rows on heel).

Turn heel as follows:

Row 1: K2, SKP, k1, turn.

Row 2: Sl 1, p3, turn.

Row 3: K3, SKP, k1, turn.

Row 4: Sl 1, p4, turn.

Row 5: K4, SKP, k1, turn.

Row 6: Sl 1, p5, turn.

Row 7: K5, SKP, k1, turn.

Row 8: Sl 1, p6, turn.

Row 9: K6, SKP, k1 (8 sts).

Break yarn.

Next: Using Aran, k across 8 sts starting on the outer edge of the RS; pick up and k 9 sts on inner edge of half heel; k across 27 sts of instep; pick up and k 9 sts on inner edge of other half heel; k across 8 sts (61 sts).

P 1 row.

Gusset and instep
Row 1: K14, k2tog, k29, SKP, k14 (59 sts).

Row 2: P.

Row 3: K13, k2tog, k29, SKP, k13 (57 sts).

Row 4: P.

Row 5: K12, k2tog, k29, SKP, k12 (55 sts).

Row 6: P.

Row 7: K11, k2tog, k29, SKP, k11 (53 sts).

Row 8: P.

Row 9: K10, k2tog, k29, SKP, k10 (51 sts).

Row 10: P.

Row 11: K9, k2tog, k29, SKP, k9 (49 sts).

Row 12: P.

K 1 row, p 1 row for 22 rows.

Row 23 (decrease row): K23, k2tog, k24 (48 sts).

Row 24: P.

Break yarn, leaving a 14in (36cm) end for sewing up.

Shape toe
Row 1: Using Cherry Red, k9, k2tog, k2, SKP, k18, k2tog, k2, SKP, k9 (44 sts).

Row 2: P.

Row 3: K8, k2tog, k2, SKP, k16, k2tog, k2, SKP, k8 (40 sts).

Row 4: P.

Row 5: K7, k2tog, k2, SKP, k14, k2tog, k2, SKP, k7 (36 sts).

Row 6: P.

Row 7: K6, k2tog, k2, SKP, k12, k2tog, k2, SKP, k6 (32 sts).

Row 8: P.

Row 9: K5, k2tog, k2, SKP, k10, k2tog, k2, SKP, k5 (28 sts).

Row 10: P.

Row 11: K4, k2tog, k2, SKP, k8, k2tog, k2, SKP, k4 (24 sts).

Row 12: P.

Row 13: K3, k2tog, k2, SKP, k6, k2tog, k2, SKP, k3 (20 sts).

Row 14: P.

Row 15: K2, k2tog, k2, SKP, k4, k2tog, k2, SKP, k2 (16 sts).

After last row, with WS facing you, place first 4 sts on a dpn. Sl next 8 sts to a second needle and sl last 4 sts to third needle.

Begin with fourth st, sl 4 sts from first needle, k last 4 sts from third needle to same needle with edges at the centre of needle. Needles should be parallel with one another.

Break yarn, leaving a 14in (36cm) length for weaving the toe.

Weaving the toe
Thread end of yarn into tapestry needle and weave sts together as follows:

Front needle: Pass needle through as if to k and sl st off, pass through second st of front needle as if to p but leave st on needle, draw yarn through.

Back needle: Pass needle through as if to p and sl st off, pass through second st of back needle as if to k but leave st on needle, draw yarn through.

Repeat until all sts are joined.

Fasten off.

Completing the stocking
Use a tapestry needle to sew in all ends securely. Weave in all ends using matching colours. Use a mattress stitch to join the seams. Sew the jingle bell onto the toe. To make a chain, use a dpn and cast on 3 sts. K each row until you have the desired length for your chain. Use a tapestry needle to sew the chain onto the top of the stocking.

Papa chart

Each square on the chart represents one stitch.

Key:

Paddy Green · Cherry Red · Aran · Petal Pink · Black · Whitey White · Grey Heather

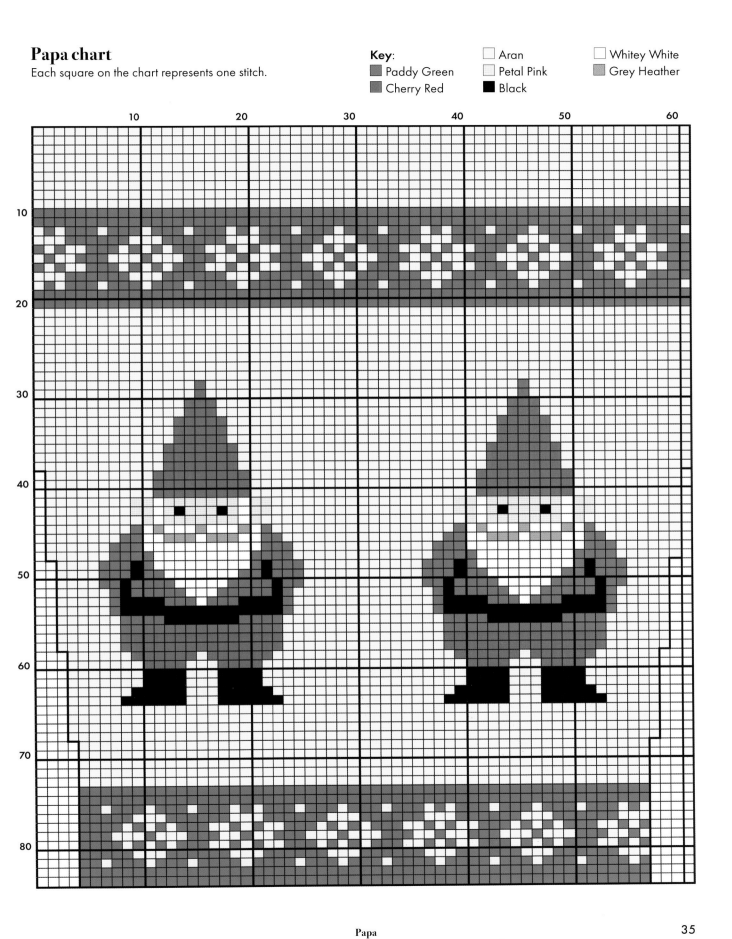

Ziggy

Skill level

Materials
- Pair of 3.5mm (US4) knitting needles
- 3.5mm (US4) double-pointed knitting needles
- Red Heart Super Saver, 100% acrylic (364yd/333m per 198g ball):
  1 x 198g ball in Cherry Red,
  Paddy Green, Aran
- Oddment of Petal Pink
- Bernat Pipsqueak, 100% polyester (101yd/92m per 100g ball):
  1 x 100g ball in Whitey White
- Tapestry needle
- 2 stitch holders
- Jingle bell (optional)

Finished size
24in (60cm) long and 7in (18cm) wide

Starting the stocking
Cast on 60 sts in Paddy Green.
Cuff
Working in k2, p2 rib, continue for 7 rows. Break yarn, leaving about 10in (25cm) for sewing up.

Personalize your stocking
If you would like a name or date on your stocking, use the alphabet and number chart provided on page 138, and a yarn colour of your choice.
Row 1: P 1 row in Aran.
Row 2: K 1 row and inc 1 st at end of row (61 sts).
Rows 3–9: Continue to p 1 row and k 1 row in Aran for 7 more rows for a total of 9 rows.

Main design

Row 10: Using st st, follow the chart opposite in Cherry Red.

Dec 1 st each side on rows 39, 49, 59 and 69 (53 sts).

Work to end of chart, end on a p row. Be sure to cross yarns when changing colours to avoid leaving a hole in the work.

Break yarn, leaving an 18in (46cm) end for sewing up.

With RS facing you, sl first 13 sts onto a stitch holder for right half of heel; sl next 27 sts onto a stitch holder for instep; sl last 13 sts onto a dpn for left half of heel.

Left half of heel

With WS facing you, k and p the following rows in Paddy Green.

First row: P.

Next row: Sl 1, k12.

Repeat these two rows for a total of 8 times (18 rows on heel).

Turn heel as follows:

Row 1: P2, p2tog, p1, turn.
Row 2: Sl 1, k3, turn.
Row 3: P3, p2tog, p1, turn.
Row 4: Sl 1, k4, turn.
Row 5: P4, p2tog, p1, turn.
Row 6: Sl 1, k5, turn.
Row 7: P5, p2tog, p1, turn.
Row 8: Sl 1, k6, turn.
Row 9: P6, p2tog, p1 (8 sts).

Break yarn, place sts on stitch holder or leave on needle.

Right half of heel

With RS facing you, k and p the following rows in Paddy Green.

First row: K.

Next row: Sl 1, p12.

Repeat these two rows for a total of 8 times (18 rows on heel).

Turn heel as follows:

Row 1: K2, SKP, k1, turn.
Row 2: Sl 1, p3, turn.
Row 3: K3, SKP, k1, turn.
Row 4: Sl 1, p4, turn.
Row 5: K4, SKP, k1, turn.
Row 6: Sl 1, p5, turn.
Row 7: K5, SKP, k1, turn.

Row 8: Sl 1, p6, turn.
Row 9: K6, SKP, k1 (8 sts).
Break yarn.

Next: Using Aran, k across 8 sts starting on the outer edge of the RS; pick up and k 9 sts on inner edge of half heel; k across 27 sts of instep; pick up and k 9 sts on inner edge of other half heel; k across 8 sts (61 sts).
P 1 row.

Gusset and instep

Row 1: K14, k2tog, k29, SKP, k14 (59 sts).
Row 2: P.
Row 3: K13, k2tog, k29, SKP, k13 (57 sts).
Row 4: P.
Row 5: K12, k2tog, k29, SKP, k12 (55 sts).
Row 6: P.
Row 7: K11, k2tog, k29, SKP, k11 (53 sts).
Row 8: P.
Row 9: K10, k2tog, k29, SKP, k10 (51 sts).
Row 10: P.
Row 11: K9, k2tog, k29, SKP, k9 (49 sts).
Row 12: P.
K 1 row, p 1 row for 22 rows.
Row 23 (decrease row): K23, k2tog, k24 (48 sts).
Row 24: P.
Break yarn, leaving a 14in (36cm) end for sewing up.

Shape toe

Row 1: Using Paddy Green, k9, k2tog, k2, SKP, k18, k2tog, k2, SKP, k9 (44 sts).
Row 2: P.
Row 3: K8, k2tog, k2, SKP, k16, k2tog, k2, SKP, k8 (40 sts).
Row 4: P.
Row 5: K7, k2tog, k2, SKP, k14, k2tog, k2, SKP, k7 (36 sts).
Row 6: P.
Row 7: K6, k2tog, k2, SKP, k12, k2tog, k2, SKP, k6 (32 sts).
Row 8: P.

Row 9: K5, k2tog, k2, SKP, k10, k2tog, k2, SKP, k5 (28 sts).
Row 10: P.
Row 11: K4, k2tog, k2, SKP, k8, k2tog, k2, SKP, k4 (24 sts).
Row 12: P.
Row 13: K3, k2tog, k2, SKP, k6, k2tog, k2, SKP, k3 (20 sts).
Row 14: P.
Row 15: K2, k2tog, k2, SKP, k4, k2tog, k2, SKP, k2 (16 sts).

After last row, with WS facing you, place first 4 sts on a dpn. Sl next 8 sts to a second needle and sl last 4 sts to third needle.

Begin with fourth st, sl 4 sts from first needle, k last 4 sts from third needle to same needle with edges at the centre of needle. Needles should be parallel with one another.

Break yarn, leaving a 14in (36cm) length for weaving the toe.

Weaving the toe

Thread end of yarn into tapestry needle and weave sts together as follows:

Front needle: Pass needle through as if to k and sl st off, pass through second st of front needle as if to p but leave st on needle, draw yarn through.

Back needle: Pass needle through as if to p and sl st off, pass through second st of back needle as if to k but leave st on needle, draw yarn through.

Repeat until all sts are joined.
Fasten off.

Completing the stocking

Use a tapestry needle to sew in all ends securely. Weave in all ends using matching colours. Use a mattress stitch to join the seams. Sew the jingle bell onto the toe. To make a chain, use a dpn and cast on 3 sts. K each row until you have the desired length for your chain. Use a tapestry needle to sew the chain onto the top of the stocking.

Ziggy chart

Each square on the chart represents one stitch.

Key:
- ■ Paddy Green
- ■ Cherry Red
- □ Aran
- ▫ Petal Pink
- □ Whitey White

Simon

Skill level

Materials
- Pair of 3.5mm (US4) knitting needles
- 3.5mm (US4) double-pointed knitting needles
- Red Heart Super Saver, 100% acrylic (364yd/333m per 198g ball):
  1 x 198g ball in Cherry Red, Paddy Green, Aran, Grey Heather
- Oddment of Petal Pink
- Bernat Pipsqueak, 100% polyester (101yd/92m per 100g ball):
  1 x 100g ball in Whitey White
- Tapestry needle
- 2 stitch holders
- Jingle bell (optional)

Finished size
24in (60cm) long and 7in (18cm) wide

Starting the stocking
Cast on 60 sts in Cherry Red.
Cuff
Working in k2, p2 rib, continue for 7 rows. Break yarn, leaving about 10in (25cm) for sewing up.

Personalize your stocking
If you would like a name or date on your stocking, use the alphabet and number chart provided on page 138, and a yarn colour of your choice.
Row 1: P 1 row in Aran.
Row 2: K 1 row and inc 1 st at end of row (61 sts).
Rows 3–9: Continue to p 1 row and k 1 row in Aran for 7 more rows for a total of 9 rows.

Main design

Row 10: Using st st, follow the chart opposite in Paddy Green.

Dec 1 st each side on rows 39, 49, 59 and 69 (53 sts).

Work to end of chart, end on a p row.

Be sure to cross yarns when changing colours to avoid leaving a hole in the work.

Break yarn, leaving an 18in (46cm) end for sewing up.

With RS facing you, sl first 13 sts onto a stitch holder for right half of heel; sl next 27 sts onto a stitch holder for instep; sl last 13 sts onto a dpn for left half of heel.

Left half of heel

With WS facing you, k and p the following rows in Cherry Red.

First row: P.

Next row: Sl 1, k12.

Repeat these two rows for a total of 8 times (18 rows on heel).

Turn heel as follows:

Row 1: P2, p2tog, p1, turn.

Row 2: Sl 1, k3, turn.

Row 3: P3, p2tog, p1, turn.

Row 4: Sl 1, k4, turn.

Row 5: P4, p2tog, p1, turn.

Row 6: Sl 1, k5, turn.

Row 7: P5, p2tog, p1, turn.

Row 8: Sl 1, k6, turn.

Row 9: P6, p2tog, p1 (8 sts).

Break yarn, place sts on stitch holder or leave on needle.

Right half of heel

With RS facing you, k and p the following rows in Cherry Red.

First row: K.

Next row: Sl 1, p12.

Repeat these two rows for a total of 8 times; 18 rows on heel.

Turn heel as follows:

Row 1: K2, SKP, k1, turn.

Row 2: Sl 1, p3, turn.

Row 3: K3, SKP, k1, turn.

Row 4: Sl 1, p4, turn.

Row 5: K4, SKP, k1, turn.

Row 6: Sl 1, p5, turn.

Row 7: K5, SKP, k1, turn.

Row 8: Sl 1, p6, turn.

Row 9: K6, SKP, k1 (8 sts).

Break yarn.

Next: Using Aran, k across 8 sts starting on the outer edge of the RS; pick up and k 9 sts on inner edge of half heel; k across 27 sts of instep; pick up and k 9 sts on inner edge of other half heel; k across 8 sts (61 sts).

P 1 row.

Gusset and instep

Row 1: K14, k2tog, k29, SKP, k14 (59 sts).

Row 2: P.

Row 3: K13, k2tog, k29, SKP, k13 (57 sts).

Row 4: P.

Row 5: K12, k2tog, k29, SKP, k12 (55 sts).

Row 6: P.

Row 7: K11, k2tog, k29, SKP, k11 (53 sts).

Row 8: P.

Row 9: K10, k2tog, k29, SKP, k10 (51 sts).

Row 10: P.

Row 11: K9, k2tog, k29, SKP, k9 (49 sts).

Row 12: P.

K 1 row, p 1 row for 22 rows.

Row 23 (decrease row): K23, k2tog, k24 (48 sts).

Row 24: P.

Break yarn, leaving a 14in (36cm) end for sewing up.

Shape toe

Row 1: Using Cherry Red, k9, k2tog, k2, SKP, k18, k2tog, k2, SKP, k9 (44 sts).

Row 2: P.

Row 3: K8, k2tog, k2, SKP, k16, k2tog, k2, SKP, k8 (40 sts).

Row 4: P.

Row 5: K7, k2tog, k2, SKP, k14, k2tog, k2, SKP, k7 (36 sts).

Row 6: P.

Row 7: K6, k2tog, k2, SKP, k12, k2tog, k2, SKP, k6 (32 sts).

Row 8: P.

Row 9: K5, k2tog, k2, SKP, k10, k2tog, k2, SKP, k5 (28 sts).

Row 10: P.

Row 11: K4, k2tog, k2, SKP, k8, k2tog, k2, SKP, k4 (24 sts).

Row 12: P.

Row 13: K3, k2tog, k2, SKP, k6, k2tog, k2, SKP, k3 (20 sts).

Row 14: P.

Row 15: K2, k2tog, k2, SKP, k4, k2tog, k2, SKP, k2 (16 sts).

After last row, with WS facing you, place first 4 sts on a dpn. Sl next 8 sts to a second needle and sl last 4 sts to third needle.

Begin with fourth st, sl 4 sts from first needle, k last 4 sts from third needle to same needle with edges at the centre of needle. Needles should be parallel with one another.

Break yarn, leaving a 14in (36cm) length for weaving the toe.

Weaving the toe

Thread end of yarn into tapestry needle and weave sts together as follows:

Front needle: Pass needle through as if to k and sl st off, pass through second st of front needle as if to p but leave st on needle, draw yarn through.

Back needle: Pass needle through as if to p and sl st off, pass through second st of back needle as if to k but leave st on needle, draw yarn through.

Repeat until all sts are joined.

Fasten off.

Completing the stocking

Use a tapestry needle to sew in all ends securely. Weave in all ends using matching colours. Use a mattress stitch to join the seams. Sew the jingle bell onto the toe. To make a chain, use a dpn and cast on 3 sts. K each row until you have the desired length for your chain. Use a tapestry needle to sew the chain onto the top of the stocking.

Simon chart

Each square on the chart represents one stitch.

Key:

- ■ Paddy Green
- ■ Cherry Red
- ☐ Aran
- ☐ Petal Pink
- ☐ Whitey White
- ▨ Grey Heather

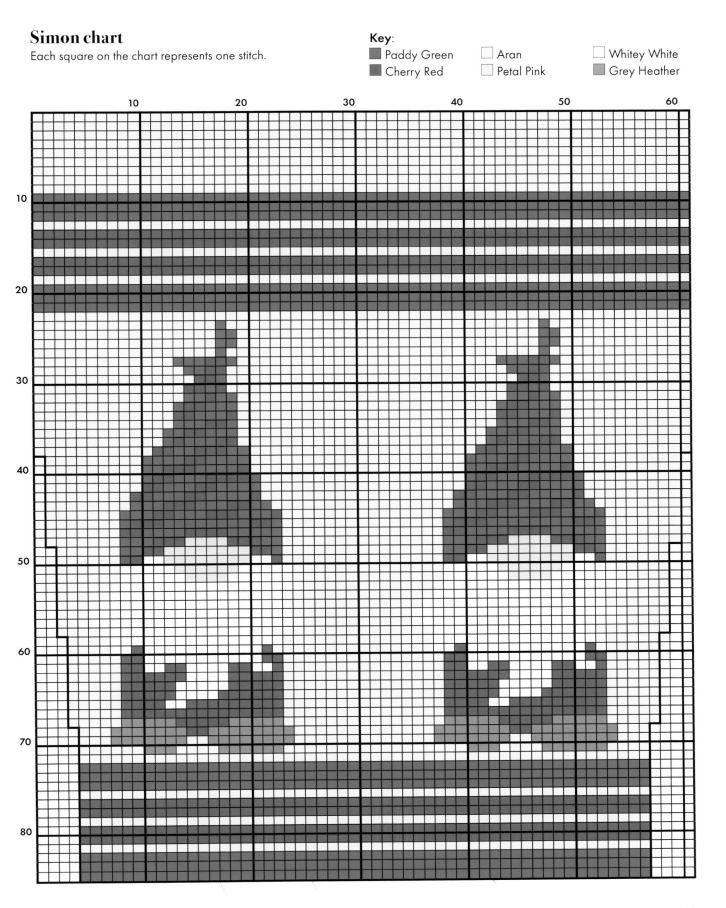

Adrian

Skill level

Materials
- Pair of 3.5mm (US4) knitting needles
- 3.5mm (US4) double-pointed knitting needles
- Red Heart Super Saver, 100% acrylic (364yd/333m per 198g ball):
  1 x 198g ball in Paddy Green, Aran, Grey Heather
- Oddment of Petal Pink
- Bernat Pipsqueak, 100% polyester (101yd/92m per 100g ball):
  1 x 100g ball in Whitey White
- Tapestry needle
- 2 stitch holders
- Jingle bell (optional)

Finished size
24in (60cm) long and 7in (18cm) wide

Starting the stocking
Cast on 60 sts in Grey Heather.
Cuff
Working in k2, p2 rib, continue for 7 rows. Break yarn, leaving about 10in (25cm) for sewing up.

Personalize your stocking
If you would like a name or date on your stocking, use the alphabet and number chart provided on page 138, and a yarn colour of your choice.
Row 1: P 1 row in Aran.
Row 2: K 1 row and inc 1 st at end of row (61 sts).
Rows 3–9: Continue to p 1 row and k 1 row in Aran for 7 more rows for a total of 9 rows.

Main design

Row 10: Using st st, follow the chart opposite in Paddy Green.

Dec 1 st each side on rows 39, 49, 59 and 69 (53 sts).

Work to end of chart, end on a p row.

Be sure to cross yarns when changing colours to avoid leaving a hole in the work.

Break yarn, leaving an 18in (46cm) end for sewing up.

With RS facing you, sl first 13 sts onto a stitch holder for right half of heel; sl next 27 sts onto a stitch holder for instep; sl last 13 sts onto a dpn for left half of heel.

Left half of heel

With WS facing you, k and p the following rows in Grey Heather.

First row: P.

Next row: Sl 1, k12.

Repeat these two rows for a total of 8 times (18 rows on heel).

Turn heel as follows:

Row 1: P2, p2tog, p1, turn.
Row 2: Sl 1, k3, turn.
Row 3: P3, p2tog, p1, turn.
Row 4: Sl 1, k4, turn.
Row 5: P4, p2tog, p1, turn.
Row 6: Sl 1, k5, turn.
Row 7: P5, p2tog, p1, turn.
Row 8: Sl 1, k6, turn.
Row 9: P6, p2tog, p1 (8 sts).

Break yarn, place sts on stitch holder or leave on needle.

Right half of heel

With RS facing you, k and p the following rows in Grey Heather.

First row: K.

Next row: Sl 1, p12.

Repeat these two rows for a total of 8 times (18 rows on heel).

Turn heel as follows:

Row 1: K2, SKP, k1, turn.
Row 2: Sl 1, p3, turn.
Row 3: K3, SKP, k1, turn.
Row 4: Sl 1, p4, turn.
Row 5: K4, SKP, k1, turn.
Row 6: Sl 1, p5, turn.
Row 7: K5, SKP, k1, turn.

Row 8: Sl 1, p6, turn.
Row 9: K6, SKP, k1 (8 sts).
Break yarn.

Next: With Aran, k across 8 sts starting on the outer edge of the RS; pick up and k 9 sts on inner edge of half heel; k across 27 sts of instep; pick up and k 9 sts on inner edge of other half heel; k across 8 sts (61 sts).

P 1 row.

Gusset and instep

Row 1: K14, k2tog, k29, SKP, k14 (59 sts).
Row 2: P.
Row 3: K13, k2tog, k29, SKP, k13 (57 sts).
Row 4: P.
Row 5: K12, k2tog, k29, SKP, k12 (55 sts).
Row 6: P.
Row 7: K11, k2tog, k29, SKP, k11 (53 sts).
Row 8: P.
Row 9: K10, k2tog, k29, SKP, k10 (51 sts).
Row 10: P.
Row 11: K9, k2tog, k29, SKP, k9 (49 sts).
Row 12: P.

K 1 row, p 1 row for 22 rows.

Row 23 (decrease row): K23, k2tog, k24 (48 sts).
Row 24: P.

Break yarn, leaving a 14in (36cm) end for sewing up.

Shape toe

Row 1: Using Grey Heather, k9, k2tog, k2, SKP, k18, k2tog, k2, SKP, k9 (44 sts).
Row 2: P.
Row 3: K8, k2tog, k2, SKP, k16, k2tog, k2, SKP, k8 (40 sts).
Row 4: P.
Row 5: K7, k2tog, k2, SKP, k14, k2tog, k2, SKP, k7 (36 sts).
Row 6: P.
Row 7: K6, k2tog, k2, SKP, k12, k2tog, k2, SKP, k6 (32 sts).
Row 8: P.

Row 9: K5, k2tog, k2, SKP, k10, k2tog, k2, SKP, k5 (28 sts).
Row 10: P.
Row 11: K4, k2tog, k2, SKP, k8, k2tog, k2, SKP, k4 (24 sts).
Row 12: P.
Row 13: K3, k2tog, k2, SKP, k6, k2tog, k2, SKP, k3 (20 sts).
Row 14: P.
Row 15: K2, k2tog, k2, SKP, k4, k2tog, k2, SKP, k2 (16 sts).

After last row, with WS facing you, place first 4 sts on a dpn. Sl next 8 sts to a second needle and sl last 4 sts to third needle.

Begin with fourth st, sl 4 sts from first needle, k last 4 sts from third needle to same needle with edges at the centre of needle. Needles should be parallel with one another.

Break yarn, leaving a 14in (36cm) length for weaving the toe.

Weaving the toe

Thread end of yarn into tapestry needle and weave sts together as follows:

Front needle: Pass needle through as if to k and sl st off, pass through second st of front needle as if to p but leave st on needle, draw yarn through.

Back needle: Pass needle through as if to p and sl st off, pass through second st of back needle as if to k but leave st on needle, draw yarn through.

Repeat until all sts are joined.

Fasten off.

Completing the stocking

Use a tapestry needle to sew in all ends securely. Weave in all ends using matching colours. Use a mattress stitch to join the seams. Sew the jingle bell onto the toe. To make a chain, use a dpn and cast on 3 sts. K each row until you have the desired length for your chain. Use a tapestry needle to sew the chain onto the top of the stocking.

Adrian chart

Each square on the chart represents one stitch.

Key:

☐ Aran
☐ Whitey White
■ Paddy Green
☐ Petal Pink
■ Grey Heather

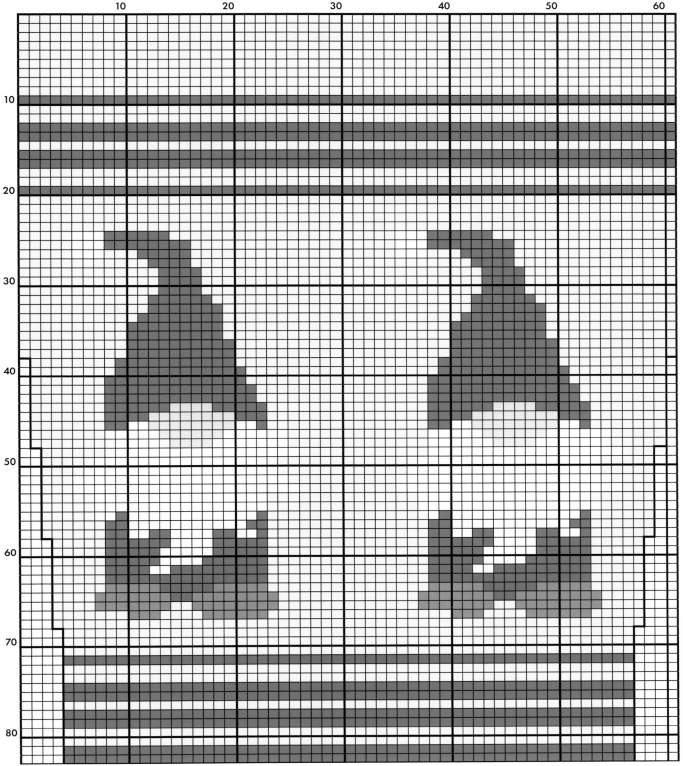

Timothy

Skill level

Materials
- Pair of 3.5mm (US4) knitting needles
- 3.5mm (US4) double-pointed knitting needles
- Red Heart Super Saver, 100% acrylic (364yd/333m per 198g ball):
  1 x 198g ball in Cherry Red, Aran, Grey Heather
- Oddment of Petal Pink
- Bernat Pipsqueak, 100% polyester (101yd/92m per 100g ball):
  1 x 100g ball in Whitey White
- Tapestry needle
- 2 stitch holders
- Jingle bell (optional)

Finished size
24in (60cm) long and 7in (18cm) wide

Starting the stocking
Cast on 60 sts in Grey Heather.
Cuff
Working in k2, p2 rib, continue for 7 rows. Break yarn, leaving about 10in (25cm) for sewing up.

Personalize your stocking
If you would like a name or date on your stocking, use the alphabet and number chart provided on page 138, and a yarn colour of your choice.
Row 1: P 1 row in Aran.
Row 2: K 1 row and inc 1 st at end of row (61 sts).
Rows 3–9: Continue to p 1 row and k 1 row in Aran for 7 more rows for a total of 9 rows.

Main design

Row 10: Using st st, follow the chart opposite in Cherry Red.

Dec 1 st each side on rows 39, 49, 59 and 69 (53 sts).

Work to end of chart, end on a p row.

Be sure to cross yarns when changing colours to avoid leaving a hole in the work.

Break yarn, leaving an 18in (46cm) end for sewing up.

With RS facing you, sl first 13 sts onto a stitch holder for right half of heel; sl next 27 sts onto a stitch holder for instep; sl last 13 sts onto a dpn for left half of heel.

Left half of heel

With WS facing you, k and p the following rows in Grey Heather.

First row: P.

Next row: Sl 1, k12.

Repeat these two rows for a total of 8 times (18 rows on heel).

Turn heel as follows:

Row 1: P2, p2tog, p1, turn.
Row 2: Sl 1, k3, turn.
Row 3: P3, p2tog, p1, turn.
Row 4: Sl 1, k4, turn.
Row 5: P4, p2tog, p1, turn.
Row 6: Sl 1, k5, turn.
Row 7: P5, p2tog, p1, turn.
Row 8: Sl 1, k6, turn.
Row 9: P6, p2tog, p1 (8 sts).

Break yarn, place sts on stitch holder or leave on needle.

Right half of heel

With RS facing you, k and p the following rows in Grey Heather.

First row: K.

Next row: Sl 1, p12.

Repeat these two rows for a total of 8 times (18 rows on heel).

Turn heel as follows:

Row 1: K2, SKP, k1, turn.
Row 2: Sl 1, p3, turn.
Row 3: K3, SKP, k1, turn.
Row 4: Sl 1, p4, turn.
Row 5: K4, SKP, k1, turn.
Row 6: Sl 1, p5, turn.
Row 7: K5, SKP, k1, turn.

Row 8: Sl 1, p6, turn.
Row 9: K6, SKP, k1 (8 sts).

Break yarn.

Next: Using Aran, k across 8 sts starting on the outer edge of the RS; pick up and k 9 sts on inner edge of half heel; k across 27 sts of instep; pick up and k 9 sts on inner edge of other half heel; k across 8 sts (61 sts).

P 1 row.

Gusset and instep

Row 1: K14, k2tog, k29, SKP, k14 (59 sts).
Row 2: P.
Row 3: K13, k2tog, k29, SKP, k13 (57 sts).
Row 4: P.
Row 5: K12, k2tog, k29, SKP, k12 (55 sts).
Row 6: P.
Row 7: K11, k2tog, k29, SKP, k11 (53 sts).
Row 8: P.
Row 9: K10, k2tog, k29, SKP, k10 (51 sts).
Row 10: P.
Row 11: K9, k2tog, k29, SKP, k9 (49 sts).
Row 12: P.

K 1 row, p 1 row for 22 rows.

Row 23 (decrease row): K23, k2tog, k24 (48 sts).
Row 24: P.

Break yarn, leaving a 14in (36cm) end for sewing up.

Shape toe

Row 1: Using Grey Heather, k9, k2tog, k2, SKP, k18, k2tog, k2, SKP, k9 (44 sts).
Row 2: P.
Row 3: K8, k2tog, k2, SKP, k16, k2tog, k2, SKP, k8 (40 sts).
Row 4: P.
Row 5: K7, k2tog, k2, SKP, k14, k2tog, k2, SKP, k7 (36 sts).
Row 6: P.
Row 7: K6, k2tog, k2, SKP, k12, k2tog, k2, SKP, k6 (32 sts).
Row 8: P.

Row 9: K5, k2tog, k2, SKP, k10, k2tog, k2, SKP, k5 (28 sts).
Row 10: P.
Row 11: K4, k2tog, k2, SKP, k8, k2tog, k2, SKP, k4 (24 sts).
Row 12: P.
Row 13: K3, k2tog, k2, SKP, k6, k2tog, k2, SKP, k3 (20 sts).
Row 14: P.
Row 15: K2, k2tog, k2, SKP, k4, k2tog, k2, SKP, k2 (16 sts).

After last row, with WS facing you, place first 4 sts on a dpn. Sl next 8 sts to a second needle and sl last 4 sts to third needle.

Begin with fourth st, sl 4 sts from first needle, k last 4 sts from third needle to same needle with edges at the centre of needle. Needles should be parallel with one another.

Break yarn, leaving a 14in (36cm) length for weaving the toe.

Weaving the toe

Thread end of yarn into tapestry needle and weave sts together as follows:

Front needle: Pass needle through as if to k and sl st off, pass through second st of front needle as if to p but leave st on needle, draw yarn through.

Back needle: Pass needle through as if to p and sl st off, pass through second st of back needle as if to k but leave st on needle, draw yarn through.

Repeat until all sts are joined.

Fasten off.

Completing the stocking

Use a tapestry needle to sew in all ends securely. Weave in all ends using matching colours. Use a mattress stitch to join the seams. Sew the jingle bell onto the toe. To make a chain, use a dpn and cast on 3 sts. K each row until you have the desired length for your chain. Use a tapestry needle to sew the chain onto the top of the stocking.

Timothy chart

Each square on the chart represents one stitch.

Key:
■ Cherry Red ☐ Aran ☐ Petal Pink ☐ Whitey White ▨ Grey Heather

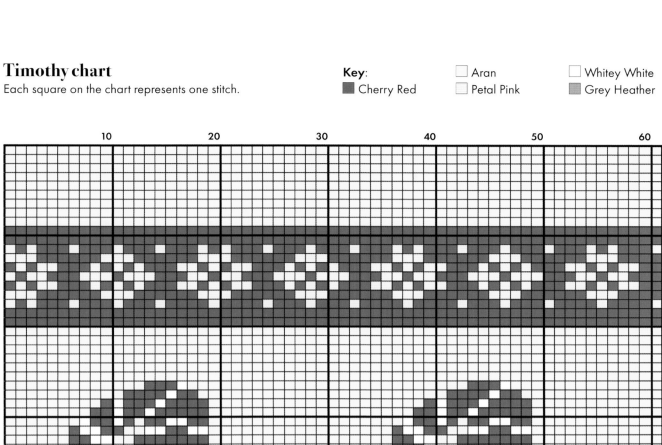

Nativity
Characters

Angel Outline

Skill level

Materials
- Pair of 3.5mm (US4) knitting needles
- 3.5mm (US4) double-pointed knitting needles
- Red Heart Super Saver, 100% acrylic (364yd/333m per 198g ball):
  1 x 198g ball in Burgundy, Aran, Black
- Oddment of Tea Leaf
- Tapestry needle
- 2 stitch holders
- Jingle bell (optional)

Finished size
23in (58cm) long and 6in (15cm) wide

Starting the stocking
Cast on 60 sts in Burgundy.
Cuff
Working in k2, p2 rib, continue for 7 rows. Break yarn, leaving about 10in (25cm) for sewing up.

Personalize your stocking
If you would like a name or date on your stocking, use the alphabet and number chart provided on page 138, and a yarn colour of your choice.
Row 1: P 1 row in any colour yarn.
Row 2: K 1 row and inc 1 st at end of row (61 sts).
Rows 3–9: Continue to p 1 row and k 1 row for 7 more rows for a total of 9 rows.

Main design

Using st st, follow the chart opposite. Dec 1 st each side on rows 39, 49, 59 and 69 as indicated on chart (53 sts). Work to end of chart, end on a p row. Be sure to cross yarns when changing colours to avoid leaving a hole in the work.

Break yarn, leaving an 18in (46cm) end for sewing up.

With RS facing you, sl first 13 sts onto a stitch holder for right half of heel; sl next 27 sts onto a stitch holder for instep; sl last 13 sts onto a dpn for left half of heel.

Left half of heel

With WS facing you, k and p the following rows in Burgundy.

First row: P.

Next row: Sl 1, k12.

Repeat these two rows for a total of 8 times (18 rows on heel).

Turn heel as follows:

Row 1: P2, p2tog, p1, turn.
Row 2: Sl 1, k3, turn.
Row 3: P3, p2tog, p1, turn.
Row 4: Sl 1, k4, turn.
Row 5: P4, p2tog, p1, turn.
Row 6: Sl 1, k5, turn.
Row 7: P5, p2tog, p1, turn.
Row 8: Sl 1, k6, turn.
Row 9: P6, p2tog, p1 (8 sts).

Break yarn, place sts on stitch holder or leave on needle.

Right half of heel

With RS facing you, k and p the following rows in Burgundy.

First row: K.

Next row: Sl 1, p12.

Repeat these two rows for a total of 8 times (18 rows on heel).

Turn heel as follows:

Row 1: K2, SKP, k1, turn.
Row 2: Sl 1, p3, turn.
Row 3: K3, SKP, k1, turn.
Row 4: Sl 1, p4, turn.
Row 5: K4, SKP, k1, turn.
Row 6: Sl 1, p5, turn.
Row 7: K5, SKP, k1, turn.
Row 8: Sl 1, p6, turn.

Row 9: K6, SKP, k1 (8 sts).
Break yarn.

Next: Using Aran, k across 8 sts starting on the outer edge of the RS; pick up and k 9 sts on inner edge of half heel; k across 27 sts of instep; pick up and k 9 sts on inner edge of other half heel; k across 8 sts (61 sts).
P 1 row.

Gusset and instep

Row 1: K14, k2tog, k29, SKP, k14 (59 sts).
Row 2: P.
Row 3: K13, k2tog, k29, SKP, k13 (57 sts).
Row 4: P.
Row 5: K12, k2tog, k29, SKP, k12 (55 sts).
Row 6: P.
Row 7: K11, k2tog, k29, SKP, k11 (53 sts).
Row 8: P.
Row 9: K10, k2tog, k29, SKP, k10 (51 sts).
Row 10: P.
Row 11: K9, k2tog, k29, SKP, k9 (49 sts).
Row 12: P.
K 1 row, p 1 row for 22 rows.
Row 23 (decrease row): K23, k2tog, k24 (48 sts).
Row 24: P.
Break yarn, leaving a 14in (36cm) end for sewing up.

Shape toe

Row 1: Using Burgundy, k9, k2tog, k2, SKP, k18, k2tog, k2, SKP, k9 (44 sts).
Row 2: P.
Row 3: K8, k2tog, k2, SKP, k16, k2tog, k2, SKP, k8 (40 sts).
Row 4: P.
Row 5: K7, k2tog, k2, SKP, k14, k2tog, k2, SKP, k7 (36 sts).
Row 6: P.
Row 7: K6, k2tog, k2, SKP, k12, k2tog, k2, SKP, k6 (32 sts).
Row 8: P.
Row 9: K5, k2tog, k2, SKP, k10, k2tog, k2, SKP, k5 (28 sts).

Row 10: P.
Row 11: K4, k2tog, k2, SKP, k8, k2tog, k2, SKP, k4 (24 sts).
Row 12: P.
Row 13: K3, k2tog, k2, SKP, k6, k2tog, k2, SKP, k3 (20 sts).
Row 14: P.
Row 15: K2, k2tog, k2, SKP, k4, k2tog, k2, SKP, k2 (16 sts).
After last row, with WS facing you, place first 4 sts on a dpn. Sl next 8 sts to a second needle and sl last 4 sts to third needle.

Begin with fourth st, sl 4 sts from first needle, k last 4 sts from third needle to same needle with edges at the centre of needle. Needles should be parallel with one another.

Break yarn, leaving a 14in (36cm) length for weaving the toe.

Weaving the toe

Thread end of yarn into tapestry needle and weave sts together as follows:

Front needle: Pass needle through as if to k and sl st off, pass through second st of front needle as if to p but leave st on needle, draw yarn through.

Back needle: Pass needle through as if to p and sl st off, pass through second st of back needle as if to k but leave st on needle, draw yarn through.

Repeat until all sts are joined.
Fasten off.

Completing the stocking

Use a tapestry needle to sew in all ends securely. Weave in all ends using matching colours. Use a mattress stitch to join the seams. Sew the jingle bell onto the toe. To make a chain, use a dpn and cast on 3 sts. K each row until you have the desired length for your chain. Use a tapestry needle to sew the chain onto the top of the stocking.

Angel Outline chart

Each square on the chart represents one stitch.

☐ Aran   ▨ Tea Leaf   ■ Black

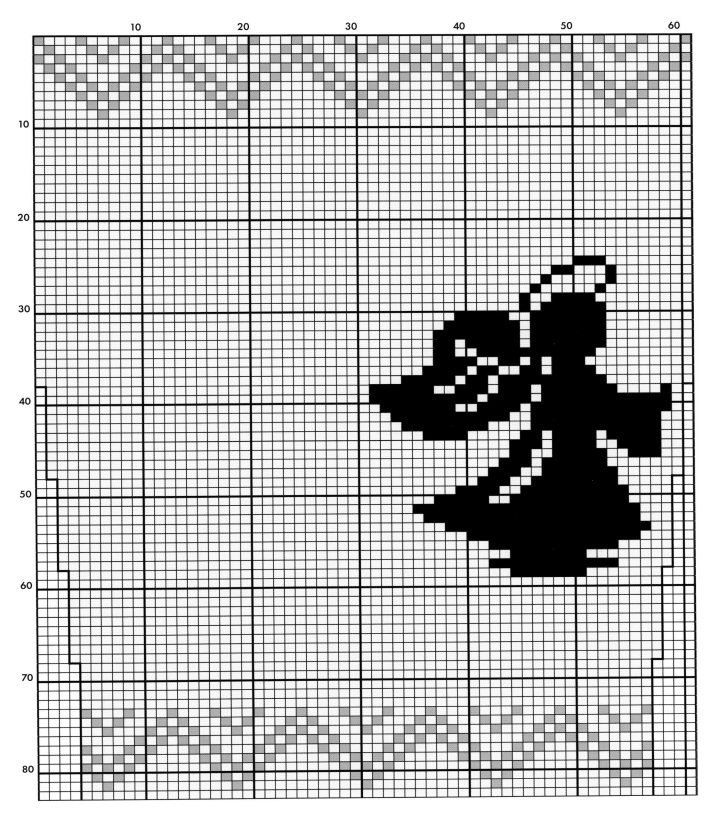

Shepherd Outline

Skill level

Materials
- Pair of 3.5mm (US4) knitting needles
- 3.5mm (US4) double-pointed knitting needles
- Red Heart Super Saver, 100% acrylic (364yd/333m per 198g ball):
  1 x 198g ball in Burgundy, Black, Aran,
- Oddment of Tea Leaf
- Tapestry needle
- 2 stitch holders
- Jingle bell (optional)

Finished size
23in (58cm) long and 6in (15cm) wide

Starting the stocking
Cast on 60 sts in Burgundy.
Cuff
Working in k2, p2 rib, continue for 7 rows. Break yarn, leaving about 10in (25cm) for sewing up.

Personalize your stocking
If you would like a name or date on your stocking, use the alphabet and number chart provided on page 138, and a yarn colour of your choice.
Row 1: P 1 row in any colour yarn.
Row 2: K 1 row and inc 1 st at end of row (61 sts).
Rows 3–9: Continue to p 1 row and k 1 row for 7 more rows for a total of 9 rows.

Main design

Using st st, follow the chart opposite. Dec 1 st each side on rows 39, 49, 59 and 69 as indicated on chart (53 sts). Work to end of chart, end on a p row. Be sure to cross yarns when changing colours to avoid leaving a hole in the work.

Break yarn, leaving an 18in (46cm) end for sewing up.

With RS facing you, sl first 13 sts onto a stitch holder for right half of heel; sl next 27 sts onto a stitch holder for instep; sl last 13 sts onto a dpn for left half of heel.

Left half of heel

With WS facing you, k and p the following rows in Burgundy.

First row: P.
Next row: Sl 1, k12.

Repeat these two rows for a total of 8 times (18 rows on heel).

Turn heel as follows:

Row 1: P2, p2tog, p1, turn.
Row 2: Sl 1, k3, turn.
Row 3: P3, p2tog, p1, turn.
Row 4: Sl 1, k4, turn.
Row 5: P4, p2tog, p1, turn.
Row 6: Sl 1, k5, turn.
Row 7: P5, p2tog, p1, turn.
Row 8: Sl 1, k6, turn.
Row 9: P6, p2tog, p1 (8 sts).

Break yarn, place sts on stitch holder or leave on needle.

Right half of heel

With RS facing you, k and p the following rows in Burgundy.

First row: K.
Next row: Sl 1, p12.

Repeat these two rows for a total of 8 times; 18 rows on heel.

Turn heel as follows:

Row 1: K2, SKP, k1, turn.
Row 2: Sl 1, p3, turn.
Row 3: K3, SKP, k1, turn.
Row 4: Sl 1, p4, turn.
Row 5: K4, SKP, k1, turn.
Row 6: Sl 1, p5, turn.
Row 7: K5, SKP, k1, turn.
Row 8: Sl 1, p6, turn.

Row 9: K6, SKP, k1 (8 sts).
Break yarn.
Next: Using Aran, k across 8 sts starting on the outer edge of the RS; pick up and k 9 sts on inner edge of half heel; k across 27 sts of instep; pick up and k 9 sts on inner edge of other half heel; k across 8 sts (61 sts).
P 1 row.

Gusset and instep

Row 1: K14, k2tog, k29, SKP, k14 (59 sts).
Row 2: P.
Row 3: K13, k2tog, k29, SKP, k13 (57 sts).
Row 4: P.
Row 5: K12, k2tog, k29, SKP, k12 (55 sts).
Row 6: P.
Row 7: K11, k2tog, k29, SKP, k11 (53 sts).
Row 8: P.
Row 9: K10, k2tog, k29, SKP, k10 (51 sts).
Row 10: P.
Row 11: K9, k2tog, k29, SKP, k9 (49 sts).
Row 12: P.
K 1 row, p 1 row for 22 rows.
Row 23 (decrease row): K23, k2tog, k24 (48 sts).
Row 24: P.
Break yarn, leaving a 14in (36cm) end for sewing up.

Shape toe

Row 1: Using Burgundy, k9, k2tog, k2, SKP, k18, k2tog, k2, SKP, k9 (44 sts).
Row 2: P.
Row 3: K8, k2tog, k2, SKP, k16, k2tog, k2, SKP, k8 (40 sts).
Row 4: P.
Row 5: K7, k2tog, k2, SKP, k14, k2tog, k2, SKP, k7 (36 sts).
Row 6: P.
Row 7: K6, k2tog, k2, SKP, k12, k2tog, k2, SKP, k6 (32 sts).
Row 8: P.
Row 9: K5, k2tog, k2, SKP, k10, k2tog, k2, SKP, k5 (28 sts).

Row 10: P.
Row 11: K4, k2tog, k2, SKP, k8, k2tog, k2, SKP, k4 (24 sts).
Row 12: P.
Row 13: K3, k2tog, k2, SKP, k6, k2tog, k2, SKP, k3 (20 sts).
Row 14: P.
Row 15: K2, k2tog, k2, SKP, k4, k2tog, k2, SKP, k2 (16 sts).

After last row, with WS facing you, place first 4 sts on a dpn. Sl next 8 sts to a second needle and sl last 4 sts to third needle.

Begin with fourth st, sl 4 sts from first needle, k last 4 sts from third needle to same needle with edges at the centre of needle. Needles should be parallel with one another.

Break yarn, leaving a 14in (36cm) length for weaving the toe.

Weaving the toe

Thread end of yarn into tapestry needle and weave sts together as follows:

Front needle: Pass needle through as if to k and sl st off, pass through second st of front needle as if to p but leave st on needle, draw yarn through.

Back needle: Pass needle through as if to p and sl st off, pass through second st of back needle as if to k but leave st on needle, draw yarn through.

Repeat until all sts are joined.
Fasten off.

Completing the stocking

Use a tapestry needle to sew in all ends securely. Weave in all ends using matching colours. Use a mattress stitch to join the seams. Sew the jingle bell onto the toe. To make a chain, use a dpn and cast on 3 sts. K each row until you have the desired length for your chain. Use a tapestry needle to sew the chain onto the top of the stocking.

Shepherd Outline chart

Each square on the chart represents one stitch.

Key:
□ Aran   ▨ Tea Leaf   ■ Black

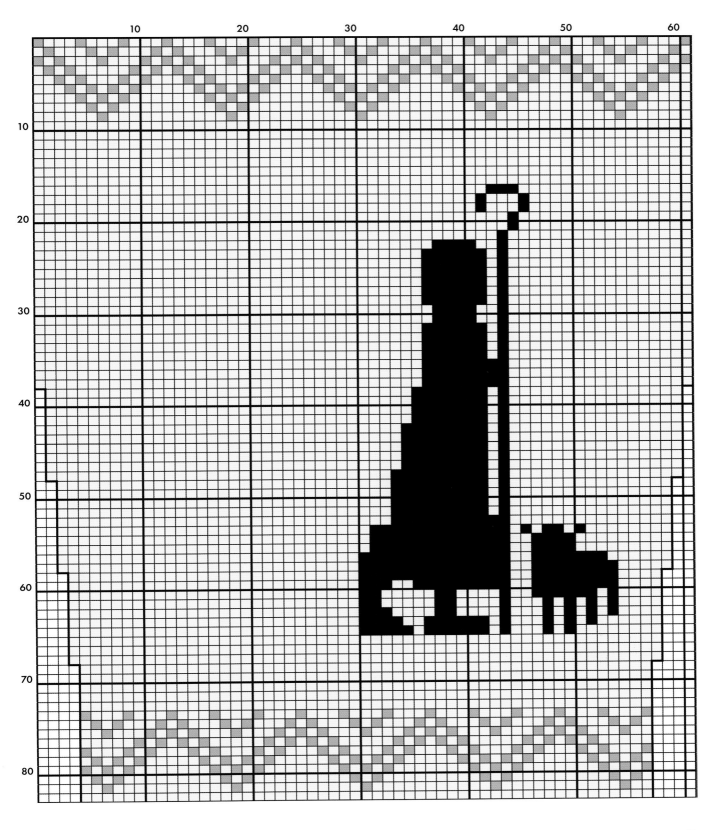

Sweet Angel

Skill level

Materials
- Pair of 3.5mm (US4) knitting needles
- 3.5mm (US4) double-pointed knitting needles
- Red Heart Super Saver, 100% acrylic (364yd/333m per 198g ball):
  1 x 198g ball in Frosty Green, Aran
- Oddments of Bright Yellow, Cafe Latte, Black, Paddy Green, Petal Pink, Cherry Red
- Tapestry needle
- 2 stitch holders
- Jingle bell (optional)

Finished size
22½in (57cm) long and 6½in (16.5cm) wide

Starting the stocking
Cast on 60 sts in Frosty Green.
Cuff
Working in k2, p2 rib, continue for 7 rows. Break yarn, leaving about 10in (25cm) for sewing up.

Personalize your stocking
If you would like a name or date on your stocking, use the alphabet and number chart provided on page 138, and a yarn colour of your choice (shown in Cherry Red) .
Row 1: P 1 row in Aran.
Row 2: K 1 row and inc 1 st at end of row (61 sts).
Rows 3–9: Continue to p 1 row and k 1 row in Aran for 7 more rows for a total of 9 rows.

Main design

Row 10: Using st st, follow the chart opposite in Frosty Green.
Dec 1 st each side on rows 39, 49, 59 and 69 (53 sts).
Work to end of chart, end on a p row.
Be sure to cross yarns when changing colours to avoid leaving a hole in the work.
Break yarn, leaving an 18in (46cm) end for sewing up.
With RS facing you, sl first 13 sts onto a stitch holder for right half of heel; sl next 27 sts onto a stitch holder for instep; sl last 13 sts onto a dpn for left half of heel.

Left half of heel

With WS facing you, k and p the following rows in Aran.
First row: P.
Next row: Sl 1, k12.
Repeat these two rows for a total of 8 times (18 rows on heel).
Turn heel as follows:
Row 1: P2, p2tog, p1, turn.
Row 2: Sl 1, k3, turn.
Row 3: P3, p2tog, p1, turn.
Row 4: Sl 1, k4, turn.
Row 5: P4, p2tog, p1, turn.
Row 6: Sl 1, k5, turn.
Row 7: P5, p2tog, p1, turn.
Row 8: Sl 1, k6, turn.
Row 9: P6, p2tog, p1 (8 sts).
Break yarn, place sts on stitch holder or leave on needle.

Right half of heel

With RS facing you, k and p the following rows in Aran.
First row: K.
Next row: Sl 1, p12.
Repeat these two rows for a total of 8 times; 18 rows on heel.
Turn heel as follows:
Row 1: K2, SKP, k1, turn.
Row 2: Sl 1, p3, turn.
Row 3: K3, SKP, k1, turn.
Row 4: Sl 1, p4, turn.
Row 5: K4, SKP, k1, turn.
Row 6: Sl 1, p5, turn.
Row 7: K5, SKP, k1, turn.

Row 8: Sl 1, p6, turn.
Row 9: K6, SKP, k1 (8 sts).
Break yarn.
Next: Using Frosty Green, k across 8 sts starting on the outer edge of the RS; pick up and k 9 sts on inner edge of half heel; k across 27 sts of instep; pick up and k 9 sts on inner edge of other half heel; k across 8 sts (61 sts).
P 1 row.

Gusset and instep

Row 1: K14, k2tog, k29, SKP, k14 (59 sts).
Row 2: P.
Row 3: K13, k2tog, k29, SKP, k13 (57 sts).
Row 4: P.
Row 5: K12, k2tog, k29, SKP, k12 (55 sts).
Row 6: P.
Row 7: K11, k2tog, k29, SKP, k11 (53 sts).
Row 8: P.
Row 9: K10, k2tog, k29, SKP, k10 (51 sts).
Row 10: P.
Row 11: K9, k2tog, k29, SKP, k9 (49 sts).
Row 12: P.
K 1 row, p 1 row for 22 rows.
Row 23 (decrease row): K23, k2tog, k24 (48 sts).
Row 24: P.
Break yarn, leaving a 14in (36cm) end for sewing up.

Shape toe

Row 1: Using Aran, k9, k2tog, k2, SKP, k18, k2tog, k2, SKP, k9 (44 sts).
Row 2: P.
Row 3: K8, k2tog, k2, SKP, k16, k2tog, k2, SKP, k8 (40 sts).
Row 4: P.
Row 5: K7, k2tog, k2, SKP, k14, k2tog, k2, SKP, k7 (36 sts).
Row 6: P.
Row 7: K6, k2tog, k2, SKP, k12, k2tog, k2, SKP, k6 (32 sts).
Row 8: P.
Row 9: K5, k2tog, k2, SKP, k10, k2tog,

k2, SKP, k5 (28 sts).
Row 10: P.
Row 11: K4, k2tog, k2, SKP, k8, k2tog, k2, SKP, k4 (24 sts).
Row 12: P.
Row 13: K3, k2tog, k2, SKP, k6, k2tog, k2, SKP, k3 (20 sts).
Row 14: P.
Row 15: K2, k2tog, k2, SKP, k4, k2tog, k2, SKP, k2 (16 sts).
After last row, with WS facing you, place first 4 sts on a dpn. Sl next 8 sts to a second needle and sl last 4 sts to third needle.
Begin with fourth st, sl 4 sts from first needle, k last 4 sts from third needle to same needle with edges at the centre of needle. Needles should be parallel with one another.
Break yarn, leaving a 14in (36cm) length for weaving the toe.

Weaving the toe

Thread end of yarn into tapestry needle and weave sts together as follows:
Front needle: Pass needle through as if to k and sl st off, pass through second st of front needle as if to p but leave st on needle, draw yarn through.
Back needle: Pass needle through as if to p and sl st off, pass through second st of back needle as if to k but leave st on needle, draw yarn through.
Repeat until all sts are joined.
Fasten off.

Completing the stocking

Use a tapestry needle to sew in all ends securely. Weave in all ends using matching colours. Use a mattress stitch to join the seams. Sew the jingle bell onto the toe. To make a chain, use a dpn and cast on 3 sts. K each row until you have the desired length for your chain. Use a tapestry needle to sew the chain onto the top of the stocking.

Sweet Angel chart

Each square on the chart represents one stitch.

Key:

- Frosty Green
- Paddy Green
- Aran
- Petal Pink
- Bright Yellow
- Black
- Cafe Latte
- Cherry Red

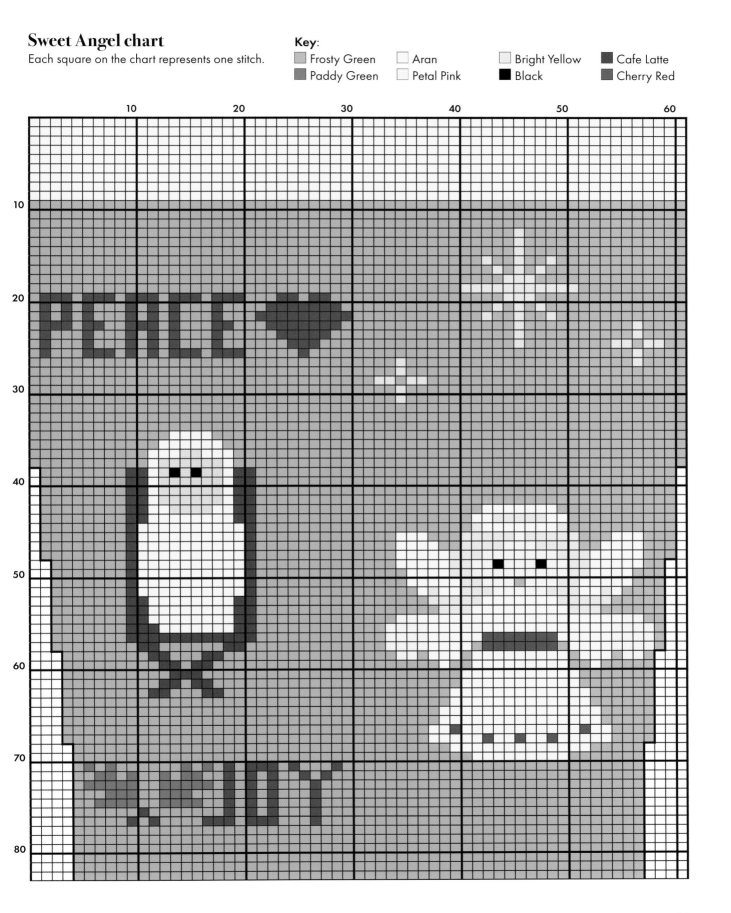

Stable Friends

Skill level

Materials
- Pair of 3.5mm (US4) knitting needles
- 3.5mm (US4) double-pointed knitting needles
- Red Heart Super Saver, 100% acrylic (364yd/333m per 198g ball):
  1 x 198g ball in Royal, Aran, Coffee, Cafe Latte
- Oddments of Grey Heather, Light Periwinkle, Black, Bright Yellow
- Tapestry needle
- 2 stitch holders
- Jingle bell (optional)

Finished size
22½in (57cm) long and 6½in (16.5cm) wide

Starting the stocking
Cast on 63 sts in Royal.
Cuff
Working in k2, p2 rib, continue for 7 rows. Break yarn, leaving about 10in (25cm) for sewing up.

Personalize your stocking
If you would like a name or date on your stocking, use the alphabet and number chart provided on page 138, and a yarn colour of your choice (shown in Light Periwinkle).
Rows 1–9: Using Aran, starting with a p row, work 9 rows in st st.

Main design

Row 10: Using st st, follow the chart opposite in Royal.

Dec 1 st each side on rows 41, 51, and 61. Dec 2 sts each side on row 71 as indicated on chart (53 sts).

Work to end of chart, end on a p row.

Be sure to cross yarns when changing colours to avoid leaving a hole in the work.

Break yarn, leaving an 18in (46cm) end for sewing up.

With RS facing you, sl first 13 sts onto a stitch holder for right half of heel; sl next 27 sts onto a stitch holder for instep; sl last 13 sts onto a dpn for left half of heel.

Left half of heel

With WS facing you, k and p the following rows in Aran.

First row: P.

Next row: Sl 1, k12.

Repeat these two rows for a total of 8 times (18 rows on heel).

Turn heel as follows:

Row 1: P2, p2tog, p1, turn.

Row 2: Sl 1, k3, turn.

Row 3: P3, p2tog, p1, turn.

Row 4: Sl 1, k4, turn.

Row 5: P4, p2tog, p1, turn.

Row 6: Sl 1, k5, turn.

Row 7: P5, p2tog, p1, turn.

Row 8: Sl 1, k6, turn.

Row 9: P6, p2tog, p1 (8 sts).

Break yarn, place sts on stitch holder or leave on needle.

Right half of heel

With RS facing you, k and p the following rows in Aran.

First row: K.

Next row: Sl 1, p12.

Repeat these two rows for a total of 8 times (18 rows on heel).

Turn heel as follows:

Row 1: K2, SKP, k1, turn.

Row 2: Sl 1, p3, turn.

Row 3: K3, SKP, k1, turn.

Row 4: Sl 1, p4, turn.

Row 5: K4, SKP, k1, turn.

Row 6: Sl 1, p5, turn.

Row 7: K5, SKP, k1, turn.

Row 8: Sl 1, p6, turn.

Row 9: K6, SKP, k1 (8 sts).

Break yarn.

Next: Using Royal, k across 8 sts starting on the outer edge of the RS; pick up and k 9 sts on inner edge of half heel; k across 27 sts of instep; pick up and k 9 sts on inner edge of other half heel; k across 8 sts (61 sts).

P 1 row.

Gusset and instep

Row 1: K14, k2tog, k29, SKP, k14 (59 sts).

Row 2: P.

Row 3: K13, k2tog, k29, SKP, k13 (57 sts).

Row 4: P.

Row 5: K12, k2tog, k29, SKP, k12 (55 sts).

Row 6: P.

Row 7: K11, k2tog, k29, SKP, k11 (53 sts).

Row 8: P.

Row 9: K10, k2tog, k29, SKP, k10 (51 sts).

Row 10: P.

Row 11: K9, k2tog, k29, SKP, k9 (49 sts).

Row 12: P.

K 1 row, p 1 row for 22 rows.

Row 23 (decrease row): K23, k2tog, k24 (48 sts).

Row 24: P.

Break yarn, leaving a 14in (36cm) end for sewing up.

Shape toe

Row 1: Using Aran, k9, k2tog, k2, SKP, k18, k2tog, k2, SKP, k9 (44 sts).

Row 2: P.

Row 3: K8, k2tog, k2, SKP, k16, k2tog, k2, SKP, k8 (40 sts).

Row 4: P.

Row 5: K7, k2tog, k2, SKP, k14, k2tog, k2, SKP, k7 (36 sts).

Row 6: P.

Row 7: K6, k2tog, k2, SKP, k12, k2tog, k2, SKP, k6 (32 sts).

Row 8: P.

Row 9: K5, k2tog, k2, SKP, k10, k2tog, k2, SKP, k5 (28 sts).

Row 10: P.

Row 11: K4, k2tog, k2, SKP, k8, k2tog, k2, SKP, k4 (24 sts).

Row 12: P.

Row 13: K3, k2tog, k2, SKP, k6, k2tog, k2, SKP, k3 (20 sts).

Row 14: P.

Row 15: K2, k2tog, k2, SKP, k4, k2tog, k2, SKP, k2 (16 sts).

After last row, with WS facing you, place first 4 sts on a dpn. Sl next 8 sts to a second needle and sl last 4 sts to third needle.

Begin with fourth st, sl 4 sts from first needle, k last 4 sts from third needle to same needle with edges at the centre of needle. Needles should be parallel with one another.

Break yarn, leaving a 14in (36cm) length for weaving the toe.

Weaving the toe

Thread end of yarn into tapestry needle and weave sts together as follows:

Front needle: Pass needle through as if to k and sl st off, pass through second st of front needle as if to p but leave st on needle, draw yarn through.

Back needle: Pass needle through as if to p and sl st off, pass through second st of back needle as if to k but leave st on needle, draw yarn through.

Repeat until all sts are joined.

Fasten off.

Completing the stocking

Use a tapestry needle to sew in all ends securely. Weave in all ends using matching colours. Use a mattress stitch to join the seams. Sew the jingle bell onto the toe. To make a chain, use a dpn and cast on 3 sts. K each row until you have the desired length for your chain. Use a tapestry needle to sew the chain onto the top of the stocking.

Stable Friends chart

Each square on the chart represents one stitch.

Key:

- ■ Royal
- ■ Black
- ■ Coffee
- ☐ Bright Yellow
- ☐ Aran
- ■ Grey Heather
- ■ Cafe Latte

Drummer Boy

Skill level
⭐⭐

Materials
- Pair of 3.5mm (US4) knitting needles
- 3.5mm (US4) double-pointed knitting needles
- Red Heart Super Saver 100% acrylic (364yd/333m per 198g): 1 x 198g ball in Delft Blue, Light Periwinkle, Soft Navy, Coffee, Aran, Cherry Red
- Oddments of Black, Bright Yellow, Petal Pink, Tea Leaf
- Tapestry needle
- 2 stitch holders
- Jingle bell (optional)

Finished size
22½in (57cm) long and 6½in (16.5cm) wide

Starting the stocking
Cast on 63 sts in Delft Blue.
Cuff
Working in k2, p2 rib, continue for 7 rows. Break yarn, leaving about 10in (25cm) for sewing up.

Personalize your stocking
If you would like a name or date on your stocking, use the alphabet and number chart provided on page 138, and a yarn colour of your choice (shown in Soft Navy).
Rows 1–9: Using Aran, starting with a p row, work 9 rows in st st.

Main design

Row 10: Using st st, follow the chart opposite in Delft Blue.

Dec 1 st each side on rows 39, 49, 59, 69 and 79 (53 sts).

Work to end of chart, end on a p row.

Be sure to cross yarns when changing colours to avoid leaving a hole in the work.

Break yarn, leaving an 18in (46cm) end for sewing up.

With RS facing you, sl first 13 sts onto a stitch holder for right half of heel; sl next 27 sts onto a stitch holder for instep; sl last 13 sts onto a dpn for left half of heel.

Left half of heel

With WS facing you, k and p the following rows in Aran.

First row: P.

Next row: Sl 1, k12.

Repeat these two rows for a total of 8 times (18 rows on heel).

Turn heel as follows:

Row 1: P2, p2tog, p1, turn.
Row 2: Sl 1, k3, turn.
Row 3: P3, p2tog, p1, turn.
Row 4: Sl 1, k4, turn.
Row 5: P4, p2tog, p1, turn.
Row 6: Sl 1, k5, turn.
Row 7: P5, p2tog, p1, turn.
Row 8: Sl 1, k6, turn.
Row 9: P6, p2tog, p1 (8 sts).

Break yarn, place sts on stitch holder or leave on needle.

Right half of heel

With RS facing you, k and p the following rows in Aran.

First row: K.

Next row: Sl 1, p12.

Repeat these two rows for a total of 8 times (18 rows on heel).

Turn heel as follows:

Row 1: K2, SKP, k1, turn.
Row 2: Sl 1, p3, turn.
Row 3: K3, SKP, k1, turn.
Row 4: Sl 1, p4, turn.
Row 5: K4, SKP, k1, turn.
Row 6: Sl 1, p5, turn.
Row 7: K5, SKP, k1, turn.

Row 8: Sl 1, p6, turn.
Row 9: K6, SKP, k1 (8 sts).
Break yarn.

Next: Using Delft Blue, k across 8 sts starting on the outer edge of the RS; pick up and k 9 sts on inner edge of half heel; k across 27 sts of instep; pick up and k 9 sts on inner edge of other half heel; k across 8 sts (61 sts).

P 1 row.

Gusset and instep

Row 1: K14, k2tog, k29, SKP, k14 (59 sts).
Row 2: P.
Row 3: K13, k2tog, k29, SKP, k13 (57 sts).
Row 4: P.
Row 5: K12, k2tog, k29, SKP, k12 (55 sts).
Row 6: P.
Row 7: K11, k2tog, k29, SKP, k11 (53 sts).
Row 8: P.
Row 9: K10, k2tog, k29, SKP, k10 (51 sts).
Row 10: P.
Row 11: K9, k2tog, k29, SKP, k9 (49 sts).
Row 12: P.
K 1 row, p 1 row for 22 rows.
Row 23 (decrease row): K23, k2tog, k24 (48 sts).
Row 24: P.

Break yarn, leaving a 14in (36cm) end for sewing up.

Shape toe

Row 1: Using Aran, k9, k2tog, k2, SKP, k18, k2tog, k2, SKP, k9 (44 sts).
Row 2: P.
Row 3: K8, k2tog, k2, SKP, k16, k2tog, k2, SKP, k8 (40 sts).
Row 4: P.
Row 5: K7, k2tog, k2, SKP, k14, k2tog, k2, SKP, k7 (36 sts).
Row 6: P.
Row 7: K6, k2tog, k2, SKP, k12, k2tog, k2, SKP, k6 (32 sts).
Row 8: P.

Row 9: K5, k2tog, k2, SKP, k10, k2tog, k2, SKP, k5 (28 sts).
Row 10: P.
Row 11: K4, k2tog, k2, SKP, k8, k2tog, k2, SKP, k4 (24 sts).
Row 12: P.
Row 13: K3, k2tog, k2, SKP, k6, k2tog, k2, SKP, k3 (20 sts).
Row 14: P.
Row 15: K2, k2tog, k2, SKP, k4, k2tog, k2, SKP, k2 (16 sts).

After last row, with WS facing you, place first 4 sts on a dpn. Sl next 8 sts to a second needle and sl last 4 sts to third needle.

Begin with fourth st, sl 4 sts from first needle, k last 4 sts from third needle to same needle with edges at the centre of needle. Needles should be parallel with one another.

Break yarn, leaving a 14in (36cm) length for weaving the toe.

Weaving the toe

Thread end of yarn into tapestry needle and weave sts together as follows:

Front needle: Pass needle through as if to k and sl st off, pass through second st of front needle as if to p but leave st on needle, draw yarn through.

Back needle: Pass needle through as if to p and sl st off, pass through second st of back needle as if to k but leave st on needle, draw yarn through.

Repeat until all sts are joined.

Fasten off.

Completing the stocking

Use a tapestry needle to sew in all ends securely. Weave in all ends using matching colours. Use a mattress stitch to join the seams. Sew the jingle bell onto the toe. To make a chain, use a dpn and cast on 3 sts. K each row until you have the desired length for your chain. Use a tapestry needle to sew the chain onto the top of the stocking.

Drummer Boy chart

Each square on the chart represents one stitch.

Key:
- Delft Blue
- Soft Navy
- Light Periwinkle
- Tea Leaf
- Coffee
- Aran
- Petal Pink
- Cherry Red
- Bright Yellow
- Black

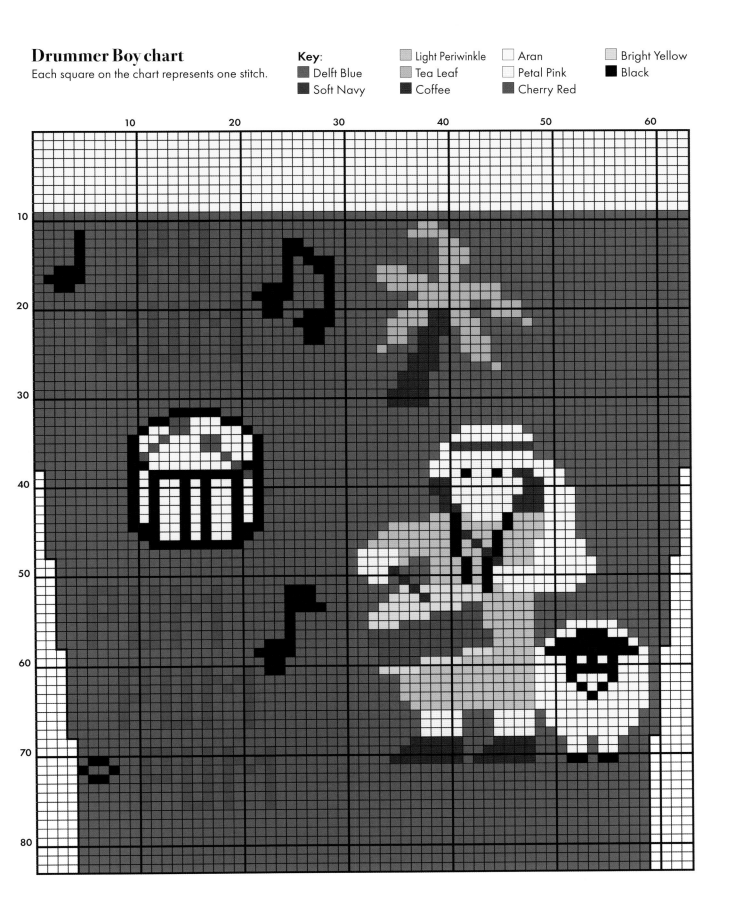

Mary and Jesus

Skill level
★ ★

Materials
- Pair of 3.5mm (US4) knitting needles
- 3.5mm (US4) double-pointed knitting needles
- Red Heart Super Saver, 100% acrylic (364yd/333m per 198g ball):
  1 x 198g ball in Aran, Tea Leaf, Bright Yellow, Light Periwinkle
- Oddments of Cafe Latte, Paddy Green, Black, Royal, Cherry Red, Petal Pink
- Tapestry needle
- 2 stitch holders
- Jingle bell (optional)

Finished size
22½in (57cm) long and 6½in (16.5cm) wide

Starting the stocking
Cast on 60 sts in Tea Leaf.
Cuff
Working in k2, p2 rib, continue for 7 rows. Break yarn, leaving about 10in (25cm) for sewing up.

Personalize your stocking
If you would like a name or date on your stocking, use the alphabet and number chart provided on page 138, and a yarn colour of your choice (shown in Paddy Green).
Row 1: P 1 row in Aran.
Row 2: K 1 row and inc 1 st at end of row (61 sts).
Rows 3–9: Continue to p 1 row and k 1 row in Aran for 7 more rows for a total of 9 rows.

Main design

Row 10: Using st st, follow the chart opposite in Tea Leaf.

Dec 1 st each side on rows 39, 49, 59 and 69 (53 sts).

Work to end of chart, end on a p row.

Be sure to cross yarns when changing colours to avoid leaving a hole in the work.

Break yarn, leaving an 18in (46cm) end for sewing up.

With RS facing you, sl first 13 sts onto a stitch holder for right half of heel; sl next 27 sts onto a stitch holder for instep; sl last 13 sts onto a dpn for left half of heel.

Left half of heel

With WS facing you, k and p the following rows in Aran.

First row: P.

Next row: Sl 1, k12.

Repeat these two rows for a total of 8 times (18 rows on heel).

Turn heel as follows:

Row 1: P2, p2tog, p1, turn.

Row 2: Sl 1, k3, turn.

Row 3: P3, p2tog, p1, turn.

Row 4: Sl 1, k4, turn.

Row 5: P4, p2tog, p1, turn.

Row 6: Sl 1, k5, turn.

Row 7: P5, p2tog, p1, turn.

Row 8: Sl 1, k6, turn.

Row 9: P6, p2tog, p1 (8 sts).

Break yarn, place sts on stitch holder or leave on needle.

Right half of heel

With RS facing you, k and p the following rows in Aran.

First row: K.

Next row: Sl 1, p12.

Repeat these two rows for a total of 8 times (18 rows on heel).

Turn heel as follows:

Row 1: K2, SKP, k1, turn.

Row 2: Sl 1, p3, turn.

Row 3: K3, SKP, k1, turn.

Row 4: Sl 1, p4, turn.

Row 5: K4, SKP, k1, turn.

Row 6: Sl 1, p5, turn.

Row 7: K5, SKP, k1, turn.

Row 8: Sl 1, p6, turn.

Row 9: K6, SKP, k1 (8 sts).

Break yarn.

Next: Using Tea Leaf, k across 8 sts starting on the outer edge of the RS; pick up and k 9 sts on inner edge of half heel; k across 27 sts of instep; pick up and k 9 sts on inner edge of other half heel; k across 8 sts (61 sts).

P 1 row.

Gusset and instep

Row 1: K14, k2tog, k29, SKP, k14 (59 sts).

Row 2: P.

Row 3: K13, k2tog, k29, SKP, k13 (57 sts).

Row 4: P.

Row 5: K12, k2tog, k29, SKP, k12 (55 sts).

Row 6: P.

Row 7: K11, k2tog, k29, SKP, k11 (53 sts).

Row 8: P.

Row 9: K10, k2tog, k29, SKP, k10 (51 sts).

Row 10: P.

Row 11: K9, k2tog, k29, SKP, k9 (49 sts).

Row 12: P.

K 1 row, p 1 row for 22 rows.

Row 23 (decrease row): K23, k2tog, k24 (48 sts).

Row 24: P.

Break yarn, leaving a 14in (36cm) end for sewing up.

Shape toe

Row 1: Using Aran, k9, k2tog, k2, SKP, k18, k2tog, k2, SKP, k9 (44 sts).

Row 2: P.

Row 3: K8, k2tog, k2, SKP, k16, k2tog, k2, SKP, k8 (40 sts).

Row 4: P.

Row 5: K7, k2tog, k2, SKP, k14, k2tog, k2, SKP, k7 (36 sts).

Row 6: P.

Row 7: K6, k2tog, k2, SKP, k12, k2tog, k2, SKP, k6 (32 sts).

Row 8: P.

Row 9: K5, k2tog, k2, SKP, k10, k2tog, k2, SKP, k5 (28 sts).

Row 10: P.

Row 11: K4, k2tog, k2, SKP, k8, k2tog, k2, SKP, k4 (24 sts).

Row 12: P.

Row 13: K3, k2tog, k2, SKP, k6, k2tog, k2, SKP, k3 (20 sts).

Row 14: P.

Row 15: K2, k2tog, k2, SKP, k4, k2tog, k2, SKP, k2 (16 sts).

After last row, with WS facing you, place first 4 sts on a dpn. Sl next 8 sts to a second needle and sl last 4 sts to third needle.

Begin with fourth st, sl 4 sts from first needle, k last 4 sts from third needle to same needle with edges at the centre of needle. Needles should be parallel with one another.

Break yarn, leaving a 14in (36cm) length for weaving the toe.

Weaving the toe

Thread end of yarn into tapestry needle and weave sts together as follows:

Front needle: Pass needle through as if to k and sl st off, pass through second st of front needle as if to p but leave st on needle, draw yarn through.

Back needle: Pass needle through as if to p and sl st off, pass through second st of back needle as if to k but leave st on needle, draw yarn through.

Repeat until all sts are joined.

Fasten off.

Completing the stocking

Use a tapestry needle to sew in all ends securely. Weave in all ends using matching colours. Use a mattress stitch to join the seams. Sew the jingle bell onto the toe. To make a chain, use a dpn and cast on 3 sts. K each row until you have the desired length for your chain. Use a tapestry needle to sew the chain onto the top of the stocking.

Mary and Jesus chart

Each square on the chart represents one stitch.

Key:
- Tea Leaf
- Aran
- Cafe Latte
- Bright Yellow
- Royal
- Light Periwinkle
- Petal Pink
- Black
- Cherry Red

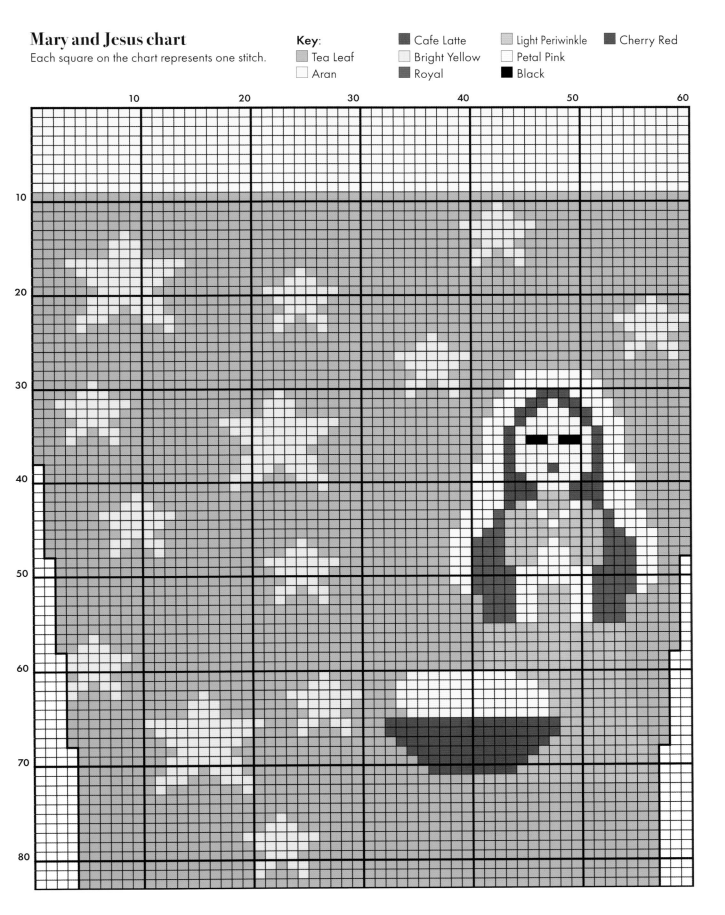

Kind Shepherd

Skill level

Materials
- Pair of 3.5mm (US4) knitting needles
- 3.5mm (US4) double-pointed knitting needles
- Red Heart Super Saver, 100% acrylic (364yd/333m per 198g ball):
  1 x 198g ball in Royal, Aran, Light Periwinkle
- Oddments of Bright Yellow, Petal Pink, Cherry Red, Coffee, Black
- Tapestry needle
- 2 stitch holders
- Jingle bell (optional)

Finished size
22½in (57cm) long and 6½in (16.5cm) wide

Starting the stocking
Cast on 60 sts in Light Periwinkle.
Cuff
Working in k2, p2 rib, continue for 7 rows. Break yarn, leaving about 10in (25cm) for sewing up.

Personalize your stocking
If you would like a name or date on your stocking, use the alphabet and number chart provided on page 138, and a yarn colour of your choice. (shown in Royal).

Row 1: P 1 row in Aran.

Row 2: K 1 row and inc 1 st at end of row (61 sts).

Rows 3–9: Continue to p 1 row and k 1 row in Aran for 7 more rows for a total of 9 rows.

Main design

Row 10: Using st st, follow the chart opposite in Light Periwinkle.

Dec 1 st each side on rows 39, 49, 59 and 69 (53 sts).

Work to end of chart, end on a p row.

Be sure to cross yarns when changing colours to avoid leaving a hole in the work.

Break yarn, leaving an 18in (46cm) end for sewing up.

With RS facing you, sl first 13 sts onto a stitch holder for right half of heel; sl next 27 sts onto a stitch holder for instep; sl last 13 sts onto a dpn for left half of heel.

Left half of heel

With WS facing you, k and p the following rows in Aran.

First row: P.

Next row: Sl 1, k12.

Repeat these two rows for a total of 8 times (18 rows on heel).

Turn heel as follows:

Row 1: P2, p2tog, p1, turn.
Row 2: Sl 1, k3, turn.
Row 3: P3, p2tog, p1, turn.
Row 4: Sl 1, k4, turn.
Row 5: P4, p2tog, p1, turn.
Row 6: Sl 1, k5, turn.
Row 7: P5, p2tog, p1, turn.
Row 8: Sl 1, k6, turn.
Row 9: P6, p2tog, p1 (8 sts).

Break yarn, place sts on stitch holder or leave on needle.

Right half of heel

With RS facing you, k and p the following rows in Aran.

First row: K.

Next row: Sl 1, p12.

Repeat these two rows for a total of 8 times (18 rows on heel).

Turn heel as follows:

Row 1: K2, SKP, k1, turn.
Row 2: Sl 1, p3, turn.
Row 3: K3, SKP, k1, turn.
Row 4: Sl 1, p4, turn.
Row 5: K4, SKP, k1, turn.
Row 6: Sl 1, p5, turn.
Row 7: K5, SKP, k1, turn.

Row 8: Sl 1, p6, turn.
Row 9: K6, SKP, k1 (8 sts).
Break yarn.

Next: Using Light Periwinkle, k across 8 sts starting on the outer edge of the RS; pick up and k 9 sts on inner edge of half heel; k across 27 sts of instep; pick up and k 9 sts on inner edge of other half heel; k across 8 sts (61 sts).
P 1 row.

Gusset and instep

Row 1: K14, k2tog, k29, SKP, k14 (59 sts).
Row 2: P.
Row 3: K13, k2tog, k29, SKP, k13 (57 sts).
Row 4: P.
Row 5: K12, k2tog, k29, SKP, k12 (55 sts).
Row 6: P.
Row 7: K11, k2tog, k29, SKP, k11 (53 sts).
Row 8: P.
Row 9: K10, k2tog, k29, SKP, k10 (51 sts).
Row 10: P.
Row 11: K9, k2tog, k29, SKP, k9 (49 sts).
Row 12: P.
K 1 row, p 1 row for 22 rows.
Row 23 (decrease row): K23, k2tog, k24 (48 sts).
Row 24: P.
Break yarn, leaving a 14in (36cm) end for sewing up.

Shape toe

Row 1: Using Aran, k9, k2tog, k2, SKP, k18, k2tog, k2, SKP, k9 (44 sts).
Row 2: P.
Row 3: K8, k2tog, k2, SKP, k16, k2tog, k2, SKP, k8 (40 sts).
Row 4: P.
Row 5: K7, k2tog, k2, SKP, k14, k2tog, k2, SKP, k7 (36 sts).
Row 6: P.
Row 7: K6, k2tog, k2, SKP, k12, k2tog, k2, SKP, k6 (32 sts).
Row 8: P.
Row 9: K5, k2tog, k2, SKP, k10, k2tog,

k2, SKP, k5 (28 sts).
Row 10: P.
Row 11: K4, k2tog, k2, SKP, k8, k2tog, k2, SKP, k4 (24 sts).
Row 12: P.
Row 13: K3, k2tog, k2, SKP, k6, k2tog, k2, SKP, k3 (20 sts).
Row 14: P.
Row 15: K2, k2tog, k2, SKP, k4, k2tog, k2, SKP, k2 (16 sts).

After last row, with WS facing you, place first 4 sts on a dpn. Sl next 8 sts to a second needle and sl last 4 sts to third needle.

Begin with fourth st, sl 4 sts from first needle, k last 4 sts from third needle to same needle with edges at the centre of needle. Needles should be parallel with one another.

Break yarn, leaving a 14in (36cm) length for weaving the toe.

Weaving the toe

Thread end of yarn into tapestry needle and weave sts together as follows:

Front needle: Pass needle through as if to k and sl st off, pass through second st of front needle as if to p but leave st on needle, draw yarn through.

Back needle: Pass needle through as if to p and sl st off, pass through second st of back needle as if to k but leave st on needle, draw yarn through.

Repeat until all sts are joined.
Fasten off.

Completing the stocking

Use a tapestry needle to sew in all ends securely. Weave in all ends using matching colours. Use a mattress stitch to join the seams. Sew the jingle bell onto the toe. To make a chain, use a dpn and cast on 3 sts. K each row until you have the desired length for your chain. Use a tapestry needle to sew the chain onto the top of the stocking.

Kind Shepherd chart

Each square on the chart represents one stitch.

Key:

- Light Periwinkle
- Royal
- Aran
- Bright Yellow
- Coffee
- Petal Pink
- Black
- Cherry Red

Three Wise Men

Skill level

Materials
- Pair of 3.5mm (US4) knitting needles
- 3.5mm (US4) double-pointed knitting needles
- Red Heart Super Saver, 100% acrylic (364yd/333m per 198g ball):
  1 x 198g ball in Soft Navy, Aran
- Oddments of Light Periwinkle, White, Cherry Red, Petal Pink, Black, Coffee, Burgundy, Bright Yellow, Tea Leaf, Royal
- Tapestry needle
- 2 stitch holders
- Jingle bell (optional)

Finished size
22½in (57cm) long and 6½in (16.5cm) wide

Starting the stocking
Cast on 60 sts in Soft Navy.
Cuff
Working in k2, p2 rib, continue for 7 rows. Break yarn, leaving about 10in (25cm) for sewing up.

Personalize your stocking
If you would like a name or date on your stocking, use the alphabet and number chart provided on page 138, and a yarn colour of your choice (shown in Light Periwinkle).
Row 1: P 1 row in Aran.
Row 2: K 1 row and inc 1 st at end of row (61 sts).
Rows 3–9: Continue to p 1 row and k 1 row in Aran for 7 more rows for a total of 9 rows.

Main design

Row 10: Using st st, follow the chart opposite in Soft Navy.

Dec 1 st each side on rows 39, 49, 59 and 69 (53 sts).

Work to end of chart, end on a p row.

Be sure to cross yarns when changing colours to avoid leaving a hole in the work.

Break yarn, leaving an 18in (46cm) end for sewing up.

With RS facing you, sl first 13 sts onto a stitch holder for right half of heel; sl next 27 sts onto a stitch holder for instep; sl last 13 sts onto a dpn for left half of heel.

Left half of heel

With WS facing you, k and p the following rows in Aran.

First row: P.

Next row: Sl 1, k12.

Repeat these two rows for a total of 8 times (18 rows on heel).

Turn heel as follows:

Row 1: P2, p2tog, p1, turn.

Row 2: Sl 1, k3, turn.

Row 3: P3, p2tog, p1, turn.

Row 4: Sl 1, k4, turn.

Row 5: P4, p2tog, p1, turn.

Row 6: Sl 1, k5, turn.

Row 7: P5, p2tog, p1, turn.

Row 8: Sl 1, k6, turn.

Row 9: P6, p2tog, p1 (8 sts).

Break yarn, place sts on stitch holder or leave on needle.

Right half of heel

With RS facing you, k and p the following rows in Aran.

First row: K.

Next row: Sl 1, p12.

Repeat these two rows for a total of 8 times (18 rows on heel).

Turn heel as follows:

Row 1: K2, SKP, k1, turn.

Row 2: Sl 1, p3, turn.

Row 3: K3, SKP, k1, turn.

Row 4: Sl 1, p4, turn.

Row 5: K4, SKP, k1, turn.

Row 6: Sl 1, p5, turn.

Row 7: K5, SKP, k1, turn.

Row 8: Sl 1, p6, turn.

Row 9: K6, SKP, k1 (8 sts).

Break yarn.

Next: Using Soft Navy, k across 8 sts starting on the outer edge of the RS; pick up and k 9 sts on inner edge of half heel; k across 27 sts of instep; pick up and k 9 sts on inner edge of other half heel; k across 8 sts (61 sts).

P 1 row.

Gusset and instep

Row 1: K14, k2tog, k29, SKP, k14 (59 sts).

Row 2: P.

Row 3: K13, k2tog, k29, SKP, k13 (57 sts).

Row 4: P.

Row 5: K12, k2tog, k29, SKP, k12 (55 sts).

Row 6: P.

Row 7: K11, k2tog, k29, SKP, k11 (53 sts).

Row 8: P.

Row 9: K10, k2tog, k29, SKP, k10 (51 sts).

Row 10: P.

Row 11: K9, k2tog, k29, SKP, k9 (49 sts).

Row 12: P.

K 1 row, p 1 row for 22 rows.

Row 23 (decrease row): K23, k2tog, k24 (48 sts).

Row 24: P.

Break yarn, leaving a 14in (36cm) end for sewing up.

Shape toe

Row 1: Using Aran, k9, k2tog, k2, SKP, k18, k2tog, k2, SKP, k9 (44 sts).

Row 2: P.

Row 3: K8, k2tog, k2, SKP, k16, k2tog, k2, SKP, k8 (40 sts).

Row 4: P.

Row 5: K7, k2tog, k2, SKP, k14, k2tog, k2, SKP, k7 (36 sts).

Row 6: P.

Row 7: K6, k2tog, k2, SKP, k12, k2tog, k2, SKP, k6 (32 sts).

Row 8: P.

Row 9: K5, k2tog, k2, SKP, k10, k2tog, k2, SKP, k5 (28 sts).

Row 10: P.

Row 11: K4, k2tog, k2, SKP, k8, k2tog, k2, SKP, k4 (24 sts).

Row 12: P.

Row 13: K3, k2tog, k2, SKP, k6, k2tog, k2, SKP, k3 (20 sts).

Row 14: P.

Row 15: K2, k2tog, k2, SKP, k4, k2tog, k2, SKP, k2 (16 sts).

After last row, with WS facing you, place first 4 sts on a dpn. Sl next 8 sts to a second needle and sl last 4 sts to third needle.

Begin with fourth st, sl 4 sts from first needle, k last 4 sts from third needle to same needle with edges at the centre of needle. Needles should be parallel with one another.

Break yarn, leaving a 14in (36cm) length for weaving the toe.

Weaving the toe

Thread end of yarn into tapestry needle and weave sts together as follows:

Front needle: Pass needle through as if to k and sl st off, pass through second st of front needle as if to p but leave st on needle, draw yarn through.

Back needle: Pass needle through as if to p and sl st off, pass through second st of back needle as if to k but leave st on needle, draw yarn through.

Repeat until all sts are joined.

Fasten off.

Completing the stocking

Use a tapestry needle to sew in all ends securely. Weave in all ends using matching colours. Use a mattress stitch to join the seams. Sew the jingle bell onto the toe. To make a chain, use a dpn and cast on 3 sts. K each row until you have the desired length for your chain. Use a tapestry needle to sew the chain onto the top of the stocking.

Three Wise Men chart

Each square on the chart represents one stitch.

Key:

- ■ Soft Navy
- ■ Royal
- ■ Light Periwinkle
- □ Aran
- ■ Cherry Red
- □ Petal Pink
- □ White
- ■ Black
- ■ Coffee
- ■ Burgundy
- □ Bright Yellow
- ■ Tea Leaf

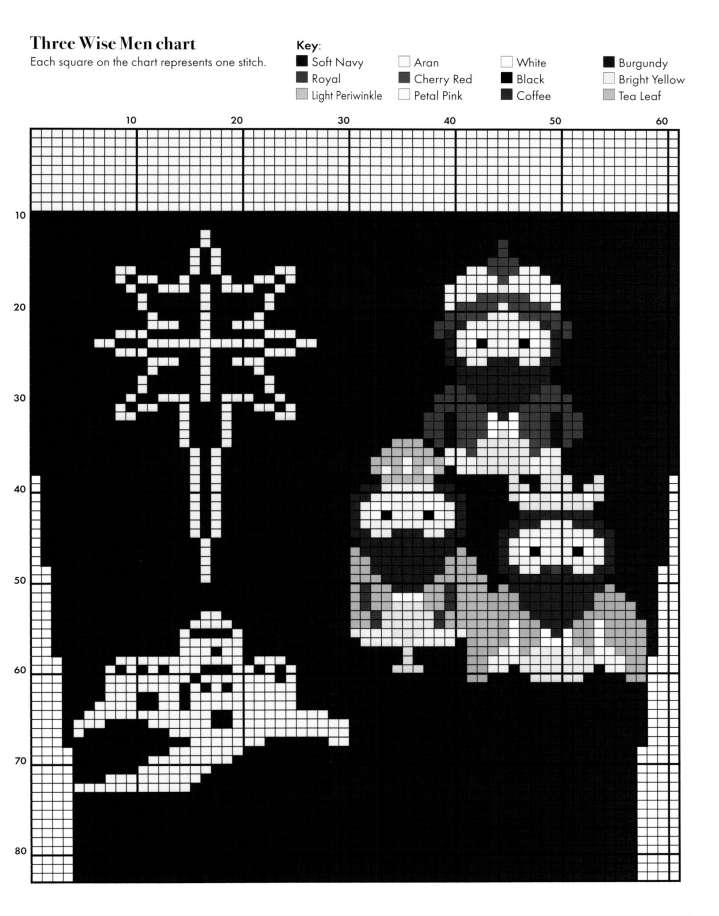

Traditional
Collection

Icy Glow

Skill level

Materials
- Pair of 3.5mm (US4) knitting needles
- 3.5mm (US4) double-pointed knitting needles
- Red Heart Super Saver, 100% acrylic (364yd/333m per 198g ball):
  1 x 198g ball in Light Periwinkle, White
- Tapestry needle
- 2 stitch holders
- Jingle bell (optional)

Finished size
23½in (60cm) long and 5in (13cm) wide

Starting the stocking
Cast on 60 sts in Light Periwinkle.
Cuff
Working in k2, p2 rib, continue for 7 rows. Break yarn, leaving about 10in (25cm) for sewing up.

Personalize your stocking
If you would like a name or date on your stocking, use the alphabet and number chart provided on page 138, and a yarn colour of your choice (shown in Light Periwinkle).
Row 1: P 1 row in any colour.
Row 2: K 1 row and inc 1 st at end of row (61 sts).
Rows 3–9: Continue to p 1 row and k 1 row for 7 more rows for a total of 9 rows.

Main design
Row 10: Using st st, follow the chart opposite.
Dec 1 st each side on rows 39, 49, 59 and 69 (53 sts).
Work to end of chart, end on a p row.
Be sure to cross yarns when changing colours to avoid leaving a hole in the work.
Break yarn, leaving an 18in (46cm) end for sewing up.
With RS facing you, sl first 13 sts onto a stitch holder for right half of heel; sl next 27 sts onto a stitch holder for instep; sl last 13 sts onto a dpn for left half of heel.

Left half of heel
With WS facing you, k and p the following rows in Light Periwinkle.
First row: P.
Next row: Sl 1, k12.
Repeat these two rows for a total of 8 times (18 rows on heel).
Turn heel as follows:
Row 1: P2, p2tog, p1, turn.
Row 2: Sl 1, k3, turn.
Row 3: P3, p2tog, p1, turn.
Row 4: Sl 1, k4, turn.
Row 5: P4, p2tog, p1, turn.
Row 6: Sl 1, k5, turn.
Row 7: P5, p2tog, p1, turn.
Row 8: Sl 1, k6, turn.
Row 9: P6, p2tog, p1 (8 sts).
Break yarn, place sts on stitch holder or leave on needle.

Right half of heel
With RS facing you, k and p the following rows in Light Periwinkle.
First row: K.
Next row: Sl 1, p12.
Repeat these two rows for a total of 8 times (18 rows on heel).
Turn heel as follows:
Row 1: K2, SKP, k1, turn.
Row 2: Sl 1, p3, turn.
Row 3: K3, SKP, k1, turn.
Row 4: Sl 1, p4, turn.
Row 5: K4, SKP, k1, turn.
Row 6: Sl 1, p5, turn.
Row 7: K5, SKP, k1, turn.

Row 8: Sl 1, p6, turn.
Row 9: K6, SKP, k1 (8 sts).
Break yarn.
Next: Rejoin Light Periwinkle, k across 8 sts starting on the outer edge of the RS; pick up and k 9 sts on inner edge of half heel; k across 27 sts of instep; pick up and k 9 sts on inner edge of other half heel; k across 8 sts (61 sts).
P 1 row.

Gusset and instep
Row 1: K14, k2tog, k29, SKP, k14 (59 sts).
Row 2: P.
Row 3: K13, k2tog, k29, SKP, k13 (57 sts).
Row 4: P.
Row 5: K12, k2tog, k29, SKP, k12 (55 sts).
Row 6: P.
Row 7: K11, k2tog, k29, SKP, k11 (53 sts).
Row 8: P.
Row 9: K10, k2tog, k29, SKP, k10 (51 sts).
Row 10: P.
Row 11: K9, k2tog, k29, SKP, k9 (49 sts).
Row 12: P.
K 1 row, p 1 row for 22 rows in White.
Row 23 (decrease row): K23, k2tog, k24 (48 sts).
Row 24: P.
Break yarn, leaving a 14in (36cm) end for sewing up.

Shape toe
Row 1: Using Light Periwinkle, k9, k2tog, k2, SKP, k18, k2tog, k2, SKP, k9 (44 sts).
Row 2: P.
Row 3: K8, k2tog, k2, SKP, k16, k2tog, k2, SKP, k8 (40 sts).
Row 4: P.
Row 5: K7, k2tog, k2, SKP, k14, k2tog, k2, SKP, k7 (36 sts).
Row 6: P.
Row 7: K6, k2tog, k2, SKP, k12, k2tog, k2, SKP, k6 (32 sts).
Row 8: P.

Row 9: K5, k2tog, k2, SKP, k10, k2tog, k2, SKP, k5 (28 sts).
Row 10: P.
Row 11: K4, k2tog, k2, SKP, k8, k2tog, k2, SKP, k4 (24 sts).
Row 12: P.
Row 13: K3, k2tog, k2, SKP, k6, k2tog, k2, SKP, k3 (20 sts).
Row 14: P.
Row 15: K2, k2tog, k2, SKP, k4, k2tog, k2, SKP, k2 (16 sts).
After last row, with WS facing you, place first 4 sts on a dpn. Sl next 8 sts to a second needle and sl last 4 sts to third needle.
Begin with fourth st, sl 4 sts from first needle, k last 4 sts from third needle to same needle with edges at the centre of needle. Needles should be parallel with one another.
Break yarn, leaving a 14in (36cm) length for weaving the toe.

Weaving the toe
Thread end of yarn into tapestry needle and weave sts together as follows:
Front needle: Pass needle through as if to k and sl st off, pass through second st of front needle as if to p but leave st on needle, draw yarn through.
Back needle: Pass needle through as if to p and sl st off, pass through second st of back needle as if to k but leave st on needle, draw yarn through.
Repeat until all sts are joined.
Fasten off.

Completing the stocking
Use a tapestry needle to sew in all ends securely. Weave in all ends using matching colours. Use a mattress stitch to join the seams. Sew the jingle bell onto the toe. To make a chain, use a dpn and cast on 3 sts. K each row until you have the desired length for your chain. Use a tapestry needle to sew the chain onto the top of the stocking.

Icy Glow chart

Each square on the chart represents one stitch.

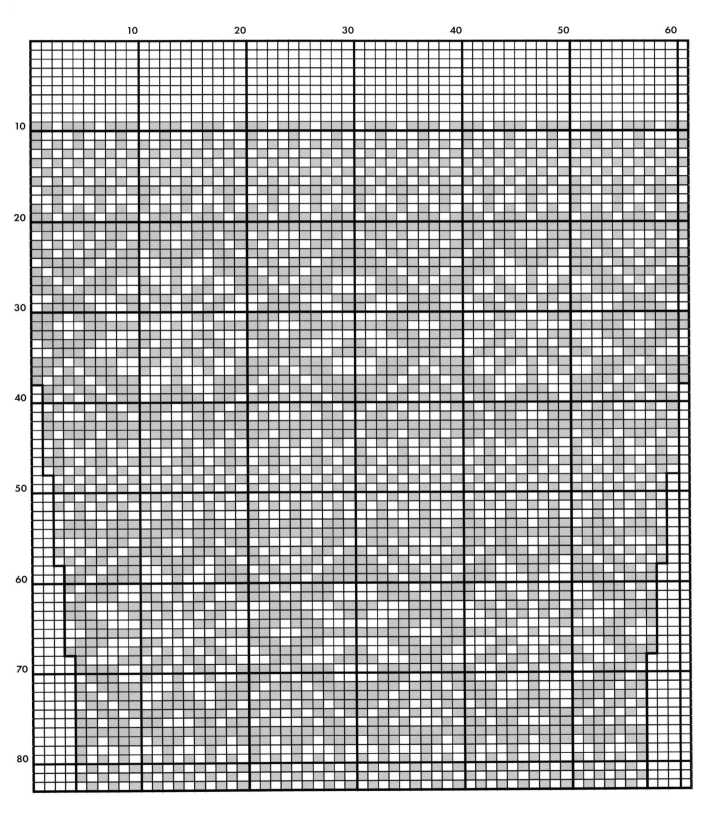

Snowfall

Skill level

Materials
- Pair of 3.5mm (US4) knitting needles
- 3.5mm (US4) double-pointed knitting needles
- Red Heart Super Saver, 100% acrylic (364yd/333m per 198g ball):
  1 x 198g ball in Grey Heather, White
- Tapestry needle
- 2 stitch holders
- Jingle bell (optional)

Finished size
23½in (60cm) long and 5in (13cm) wide

Starting the stocking
Cast on 60 sts in Grey Heather.
Cuff
Working in k2, p2 rib, continue for 7 rows. Break yarn, leaving about 10in (25cm) for sewing up.

Personalize your stocking
If you would like a name or date on your stocking, use the alphabet and number chart provided on page 138, and a yarn colour of your choice (shown in Grey Heather).
Row 1: P 1 row in any colour.
Row 2: K 1 row and inc 1 st at end of row (61 sts).
Rows 3–9: Continue to p 1 row and k 1 row for 7 more rows for a total of 9 rows.

Main design

Row 10: Using st st, follow the chart opposite.

Dec 1 st each side on rows 39, 49, 59 and 69 (53 sts).

Work to end of chart, end on a p row. Be sure to cross yarns when changing colours to avoid leaving a hole in the work.

Break yarn, leaving an 18in (46cm) end for sewing up.

With RS facing you, sl first 13 sts onto a stitch holder for right half of heel; sl next 27 sts onto a stitch holder for instep; sl last 13 sts onto a dpn for left half of heel.

Left half of heel

With WS facing you, k and p the following rows in Grey Heather.

First row: P.

Next row: Sl 1, k12.

Repeat these two rows for a total of 8 times (18 rows on heel).

Turn heel as follows:

Row 1: P2, p2tog, p1, turn.

Row 2: Sl 1, k3, turn.

Row 3: P3, p2tog, p1, turn.

Row 4: Sl 1, k4, turn.

Row 5: P4, p2tog, p1, turn.

Row 6: Sl 1, k5, turn.

Row 7: P5, p2tog, p1, turn.

Row 8: Sl 1, k6, turn.

Row 9: P6, p2tog, p1 (8 sts).

Break yarn, place sts on stitch holder or leave on needle.

Right half of heel

With RS facing you, k and p the following rows in Grey Heather.

First row: K.

Next row: Sl 1, p12.

Repeat these two rows for a total of 8 times (18 rows on heel).

Turn heel as follows:

Row 1: K2, SKP, k1, turn.

Row 2: Sl 1, p3, turn.

Row 3: K3, SKP, k1, turn.

Row 4: Sl 1, p4, turn.

Row 5: K4, SKP, k1, turn.

Row 6: Sl 1, p5, turn.

Row 7: K5, SKP, k1, turn.

Row 8: Sl 1, p6, turn.

Row 9: K6, SKP, k1 (8 sts).

Break yarn.

Next: Rejoin Grey Heather, k across 8 sts starting on the outer edge of the RS; pick up and k 9 sts on inner edge of half heel; k across 27 sts of instep; pick up and k 9 sts on inner edge of other half heel; k across 8 sts (61 sts).

P 1 row.

Gusset and instep

Row 1: K14, k2tog, k29, SKP, k14 (59 sts).

Row 2: P.

Row 3: K13, k2tog, k29, SKP, k13 (57 sts).

Row 4: P.

Row 5: K12, k2tog, k29, SKP, k12 (55 sts).

Row 6: P.

Row 7: K11, k2tog, k29, SKP, k11 (53 sts).

Row 8: P.

Row 9: K10, k2tog, k29, SKP, k10 (51 sts).

Row 10: P.

Row 11: K9, k2tog, k29, SKP, k9 (49 sts).

Row 12: P.

K 1 row, p 1 row for 22 rows in White.

Row 23 (decrease row): K23, k2tog, k24 (48 sts).

Row 24: P.

Break yarn, leaving a 14in (36cm) end for sewing up.

Shape toe

Row 1: Using Grey Heather, k9, k2tog, k2, SKP, k18, k2tog, k2, SKP, k9 (44 sts).

Row 2: P.

Row 3: K8, k2tog, k2, SKP, k16, k2tog, k2, SKP, k8 (40 sts).

Row 4: P.

Row 5: K7, k2tog, k2, SKP, k14, k2tog, k2, SKP, k7 (36 sts).

Row 6: P.

Row 7: K6, k2tog, k2, SKP, k12, k2tog, k2, SKP, k6 (32 sts).

Row 8: P.

Row 9: K5, k2tog, k2, SKP, k10, k2tog, k2, SKP, k5 (28 sts).

Row 10: P.

Row 11: K4, k2tog, k2, SKP, k8, k2tog, k2, SKP, k4 (24 sts).

Row 12: P.

Row 13: K3, k2tog, k2, SKP, k6, k2tog, k2, SKP, k3 (20 sts).

Row 14: P.

Row 15: K2, k2tog, k2, SKP, k4, k2tog, k2, SKP, k2 (16 sts).

After last row, with WS facing you, place first 4 sts on a dpn. Sl next 8 sts to a second needle and sl last 4 sts to third needle.

Begin with fourth st, sl 4 sts from first needle, k last 4 sts from third needle to same needle with edges at the centre of needle. Needles should be parallel with one another.

Break yarn, leaving a 14in (36cm) length for weaving the toe.

Weaving the toe

Thread end of yarn into tapestry needle and weave sts together as follows:

Front needle: Pass needle through as if to k and sl st off, pass through second st of front needle as if to p but leave st on needle, draw yarn through.

Back needle: Pass needle through as if to p and sl st off, pass through second st of back needle as if to k but leave st on needle, draw yarn through.

Repeat until all sts are joined.

Fasten off.

Completing the stocking

Use a tapestry needle to sew in all ends securely. Weave in all ends using matching colours. Use a mattress stitch to join the seams. Sew the jingle bell onto the toe. To make a chain, use a dpn and cast on 3 sts. K each row until you have the desired length for your chain. Use a tapestry needle to sew the chain onto the top of the stocking.

Snowfall chart

Each square on the chart represents one stitch.

Key:

☐ White ☐ Grey Heather

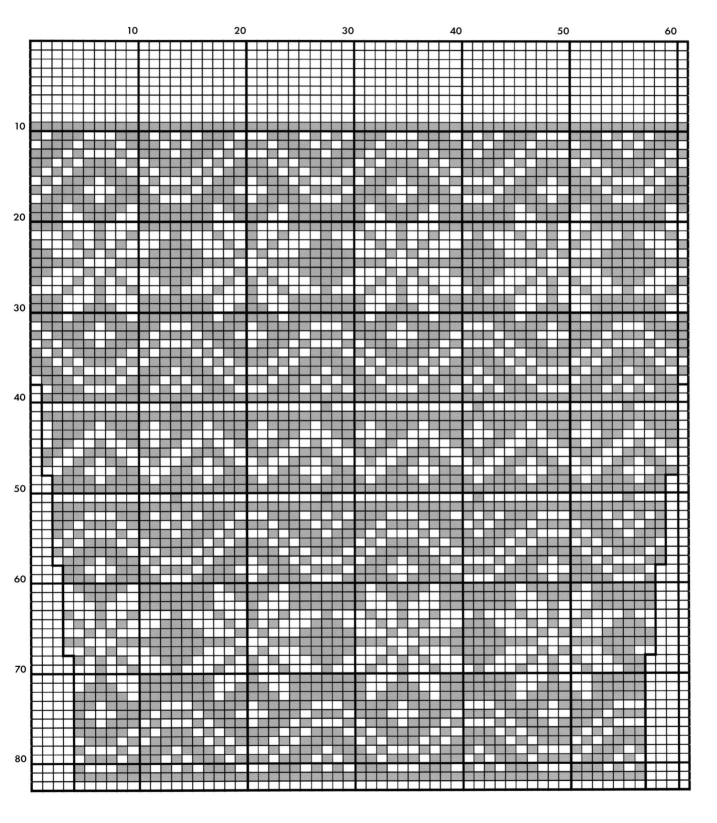

Christmas Hearts

Skill level

Materials
- Pair of 3.5mm (US4) knitting needles
- 3.5mm (US4) double-pointed knitting needles
- Red Heart Super Saver, 100% acrylic (364yd/333m per 198g ball):
  1 x 198g ball in Burgundy, Aran, Cherry Red, Paddy Green
- Oddments of Grey Heather, Light Sage, Black, Shocking Pink
- Tapestry needle
- 2 stitch holders
- Jingle bell (optional)

Finished size
22in (56cm) long and 6in (15cm) wide

Starting the stocking
Cast on 60 sts in Burgundy.
Cuff
Working in k2, p2 rib, continue for 7 rows. Break yarn, leaving about 10in (25cm) for sewing up.

Personalize your stocking
If you would like a name or date on your stocking, use the alphabet and number chart provided on page 138, and a yarn colour of your choice (shown in Cherry Red).
Row 1: P 1 row in Aran.
Row 2: K 1 row and inc 1 st at end of row (61 sts).
Rows 3–9: Continue to p 1 row and k 1 row in Aran for 7 more rows for a total of 9 rows.

Main design

Row 10: Using st st, follow chart 1 on page 100.

Dec 1 st each side on rows 39, 49, 59 and 69 (53 sts).

Work to end of chart 1, end on a p row. Be sure to cross yarns when changing colours to avoid leaving a hole in the work.

Break yarn leaving an 18in (46cm) end for sewing up.

With RS facing you, sl first 13 sts onto a stitch holder for right half of heel; sl next 27 sts onto a stitch holder for instep; sl last 13 sts onto a dpn for left half of heel.

Left half of heel

With WS facing you, k and p the following rows in Burgundy.

First row: P.

Next row: Sl 1, k12.

Repeat these two rows for a total of 8 times (18 rows on heel).

Turn heel as follows:

Row 1: P2, p2tog, p1, turn.
Row 2: Sl 1, k3, turn.
Row 3: P3, p2tog, p1, turn.
Row 4: Sl 1, k4, turn.
Row 5: P4, p2tog, p1, turn.
Row 6: Sl 1, k5, turn.
Row 7: P5, p2tog, p1, turn.
Row 8: Sl 1, k6, turn.
Row 9: P6, p2tog, p1 (8 sts).

Break yarn, place sts on stitch holder or leave on needle.

Right half of heel

With RS facing you, k and p the following rows in Burgundy.

First row: K.

Next row: Sl 1, p12.

Repeat these two rows for a total of 8 times (18 rows on heel).

Turn heel as follows:

Row 1: K2, SKP, k1, turn.
Row 2: Sl 1, p3, turn.
Row 3: K3, SKP, k1, turn.
Row 4: Sl 1, p4, turn.
Row 5: K4, SKP, k1, turn.
Row 6: Sl 1, p5, turn.
Row 7: K5, SKP, k1, turn.

Row 8: Sl 1, p6, turn.
Row 9: K6, SKP, k1 (8 sts).
Break yarn.

Next: Using Burgundy, k across 8 sts starting on the outer edge of the RS; pick up and k 9 sts on inner edge of half heel. Follow chart 2 on page 101 and k across 27 sts of instep in stocking design; pick up and k 9 sts in Burgundy on inner edge of other half heel; k across 8 sts in Burgundy (61 sts). P 1 row in same way as above.

Gusset and instep

Row 1: K14, k2tog, k29, SKP, k14 (59 sts).
Row 2: P.
Row 3: K13, k2tog, k29, SKP, k13 (57 sts).
Row 4: P.
Row 5: K12, k2tog, k29, SKP, k12 (55 sts).
Row 6: P.
Row 7: K11, k2tog, k29, SKP, k11 (53 sts).
Row 8: P.
Row 9: K10, k2tog, k29, SKP, k10 (51 sts).
Row 10: P.
Row 11: K9, k2tog, k29, SKP, k9 (49 sts).
Row 12: P.

Follow chart 2 and k 1 row, p 1 row for 22 rows.

Row 23 (decrease row): Continue to follow chart 2, k23, k2tog, k24 (48 sts).
Row 24: P.

Break yarn, leaving a 14in (36cm) end for sewing up.

Shape toe

Row 1: Using Burgundy, k9, k2tog, k2, SKP, k18, k2tog, k2, SKP, k9 (44 sts).
Row 2: P.
Row 3: K8, k2tog, k2, SKP, k16, k2tog, k2, SKP, k8 (40 sts).
Row 4: P.
Row 5: K7, k2tog, k2, SKP, k14, k2tog, k2, SKP, k7 (36 sts).
Row 6: P.
Row 7: K6, k2tog, k2, SKP, k12, k2tog,

k2, SKP, k6 (32 sts).
Row 8: P.
Row 9: K5, k2tog, k2, SKP, k10, k2tog, k2, SKP, k5 (28 sts).
Row 10: P.
Row 11: K4, k2tog, k2, SKP, k8, k2tog, k2, SKP, k4 (24 sts).
Row 12: P.
Row 13: K3, k2tog, k2, SKP, k6, k2tog, k2, SKP, k3 (20 sts).
Row 14: P.
Row 15: K2, k2tog, k2, SKP, k4, k2tog, k2, SKP, k2 (16 sts).

After last row, with WS facing you, place first 4 sts on a dpn. Sl next 8 sts to a second needle and sl last 4 sts to third needle.

Begin with fourth st, sl 4 sts from first needle, k last 4 sts from third needle to same needle with edges at the centre of needle. Needles should be parallel with one another.

Break yarn, leaving a 14in (36cm) length for weaving the toe.

Weaving the toe

Thread end of yarn into tapestry needle and weave sts together as follows:

Front needle: Pass needle through as if to k and sl st off, pass through second st of front needle as if to p but leave st on needle, draw yarn through.

Back needle: Pass needle through as if to p and sl st off, pass through second st of back needle as if to k but leave st on needle, draw yarn through.

Repeat until all sts are joined.

Fasten off.

Completing the stocking

Use a tapestry needle to sew in all ends securely. Weave in all ends using matching colours. Use a mattress stitch to join the seams. Sew the jingle bell onto the toe. To make a chain, use a dpn and cast on 3 sts. K each row until you have the desired length for your chain. Use a tapestry needle to sew the chain onto the top of the stocking.

Christmas Hearts charts

Each square on the chart represents one stitch.

Key:

■ Burgundy   ■ Cherry Red   ■ Grey Heather   ▨ Light Sage
□ Aran   ■ Black   ▨ Shocking Pink ■ Paddy Green

Chart 1

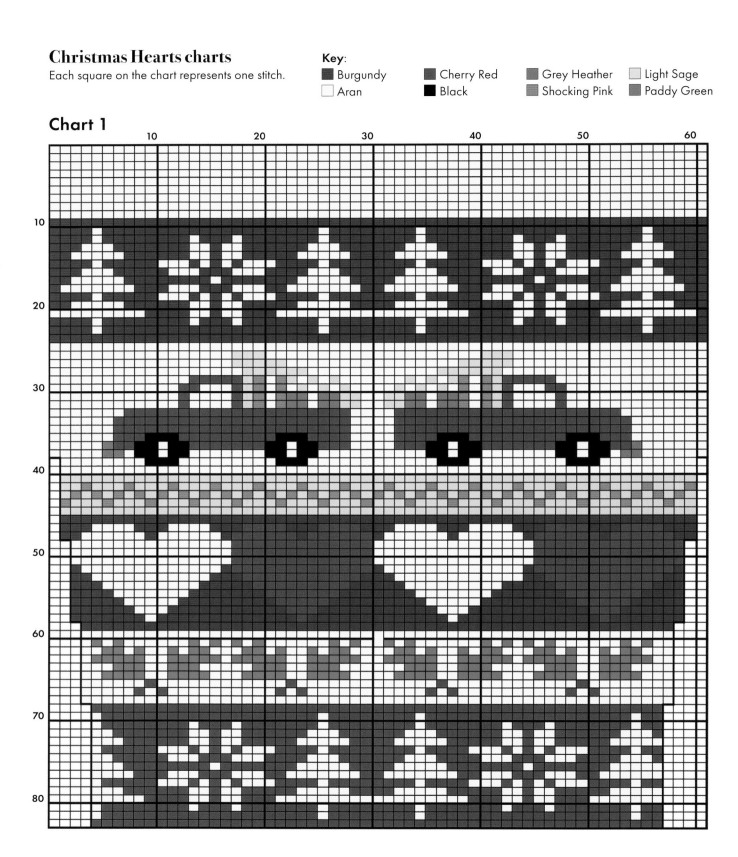

Chart 2

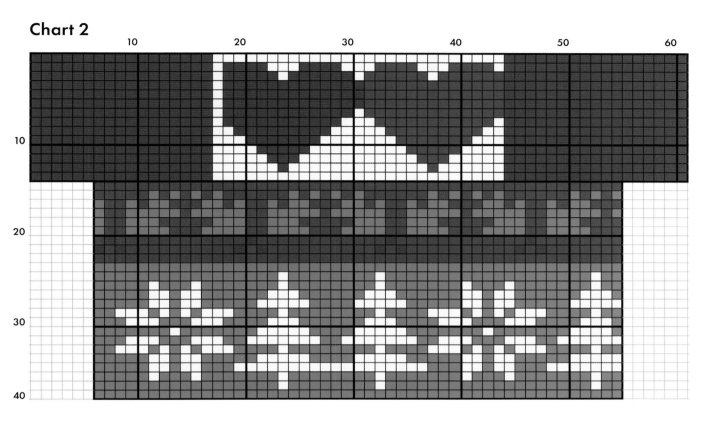

Christmas Gifts

Skill level

Materials
- Pair of 3.5mm (US4) knitting needles
- 3.5mm (US4) double-pointed knitting needles
- Red Heart Super Saver, 100% acrylic (364yd/333m per 198g ball):
  1 x 198g ball in Tea Leaf, Aran, Cherry Red, Paddy Green, White
- Tapestry needle
- 2 stitch holders
- Jingle bell (optional)

Finished size
22in (56cm) long and 6in (15cm) wide

Starting the stocking
Cast on 60 sts in Tea Leaf.
Cuff
Working in k2, p2 rib, continue for 7 rows. Break yarn, leaving about 10in (25cm) for sewing up.

Personalize your stocking
If you would like a name or date on your stocking, use the alphabet and number chart provided on page 138, and a yarn colour of your choice (shown in Cherry Red).
Row 1: P 1 row in Aran.
Row 2: K 1 row and inc 1 st at end of row (61 sts).
Rows 3–9: Continue to p 1 row and k 1 row in Aran for 7 more rows for a total of 9 rows.

Main design

Row 10: Using st st, follow chart 1 on page 106.

Dec 1 st each side on rows 39, 49, 59 and 69 (53 sts).

Work to end of chart 1, end on a p row. Be sure to cross yarns when changing colours to avoid leaving a hole in the work.

Break yarn leaving an 18in (46cm) end for sewing up.

With RS facing you, sl first 13 sts onto a stitch holder for right half of heel; sl next 27 sts onto a stitch holder for instep; sl last 13 sts onto a dpn for left half of heel.

Left half of heel

With WS facing you, k and p the following rows in Tea Leaf.

First row: P.

Next row: Sl 1, k12.

Repeat these two rows for a total of 8 times (18 rows on heel).

Turn heel as follows:

Row 1: P2, p2tog, p1, turn.

Row 2: Sl 1, k3, turn.

Row 3: P3, p2tog, p1, turn.

Row 4: Sl 1, k4, turn.

Row 5: P4, p2tog, p1, turn.

Row 6: Sl 1, k5, turn.

Row 7: P5, p2tog, p1, turn.

Row 8: Sl 1, k6, turn.

Row 9: P6, p2tog, p1 (8 sts).

Break yarn, place sts on stitch holder or leave on needle.

Right half of heel

With RS facing you, k and p the following rows in Tea Leaf.

First row: K.

Next row: Sl 1, p12.

Repeat these two rows for a total of 8 times (18 rows on heel).

Turn heel as follows:

Row 1: K2, SKP, k1, turn.

Row 2: Sl 1, p3, turn.

Row 3: K3, SKP, k1, turn.

Row 4: Sl 1, p4, turn.

Row 5: K4, SKP, k1, turn.

Row 6: Sl 1, p5, turn.

Row 7: K5, SKP, k1, turn.

Row 8: Sl 1, p6, turn.

Row 9: K6, SKP, k1 (8 sts).

Break yarn.

Next: Using Tea Leaf, k across 8 sts starting on the outer edge of the RS; pick up and k 9 sts on inner edge of half heel. Follow chart 2 on page 107 and k across 27 sts of instep in stocking design; pick up and k 9 sts in Tea Leaf on inner edge of other half heel; k across 8 sts in Tea Leaf (61 sts). P 1 row in same way as above.

Gusset and instep

Row 1: K14, k2tog, k29, SKP, k14 (59 sts).

Row 2: P.

Row 3: K13, k2tog, k29, SKP, k13 (57 sts).

Row 4: P.

Row 5: K12, k2tog, k29, SKP, k12 (55 sts).

Row 6: P.

Row 7: K11, k2tog, k29, SKP, k11 (53 sts).

Row 8: P.

Row 9: K10, k2tog, k29, SKP, k10 (51 sts).

Row 10: P.

Row 11: K9, k2tog, k29, SKP, k9 (49 sts).

Row 12: P.

Follow chart 2 and k 1 row, p 1 row for 20 rows.

Row 21 (decrease row): Continue to follow chart 2, k23, k2tog, k24 (48 sts).

Row 22: P.

Break yarn leaving a 14in (36cm) end for sewing up.

Shape toe

Row 1: Using Tea Leaf, k9, k2tog, k2, SKP, k18, k2tog, k2, SKP, k9 (44 sts).

Row 2: P.

Row 3: K8, k2tog, k2, SKP, k16, k2tog, k2, SKP, k8 (40 sts).

Row 4: P.

Row 5: K7, k2tog, k2, SKP, k14, k2tog, k2, SKP, k7 (36 sts).

Row 6: P.

Row 7: K6, k2tog, k2, SKP, k12, k2tog, k2, SKP, k6 (32 sts).

Row 8: P.

Row 9: K5, k2tog, k2, SKP, k10, k2tog, k2, SKP, k5 (28 sts).

Row 10: P.

Row 11: K4, k2tog, k2, SKP, k8, k2tog, k2, SKP, k4 (24 sts).

Row 12: P.

Row 13: K3, k2tog, k2, SKP, k6, k2tog, k2, SKP, k3 (20 sts).

Row 14: P.

Row 15: K2, k2tog, k2, SKP, k4, k2tog, k2, SKP, k2 (16 sts).

After last row, with WS facing you, place first 4 sts on a dpn. Sl next 8 sts to a second needle and sl last 4 sts to third needle.

Begin with fourth st, sl 4 sts from first needle, k last 4 sts from third needle to same needle with edges at the centre of needle. Needles should be parallel with one another. Break yarn, leaving a 14in (36cm) length for weaving the toe.

Weaving the toe

Thread end of yarn into tapestry needle and weave sts together as follows:

Front needle: Pass needle through as if to k and sl st off, pass through second st of front needle as if to p but leave st on needle, draw yarn through.

Back needle: Pass needle through as if to p and sl st off, pass through second st of back needle as if to k but leave st on needle, draw yarn through.

Repeat until all sts are joined.

Fasten off.

Completing the stocking

Use a tapestry needle to sew in all ends securely. Weave in all ends using matching colours. Use a mattress stitch to join the seams. Sew jingle bell onto the toe. To make a chain, use a dpn and cast on 3 sts. K each row until you have the desired length for your chain. Use a tapestry needle to sew the chain onto the top of the stocking.

Christmas Gifts charts

Each square on the chart represents one stitch.

Key:
- Tea Leaf
- Cherry Red
- Aran
- Paddy Green
- White

Chart 1

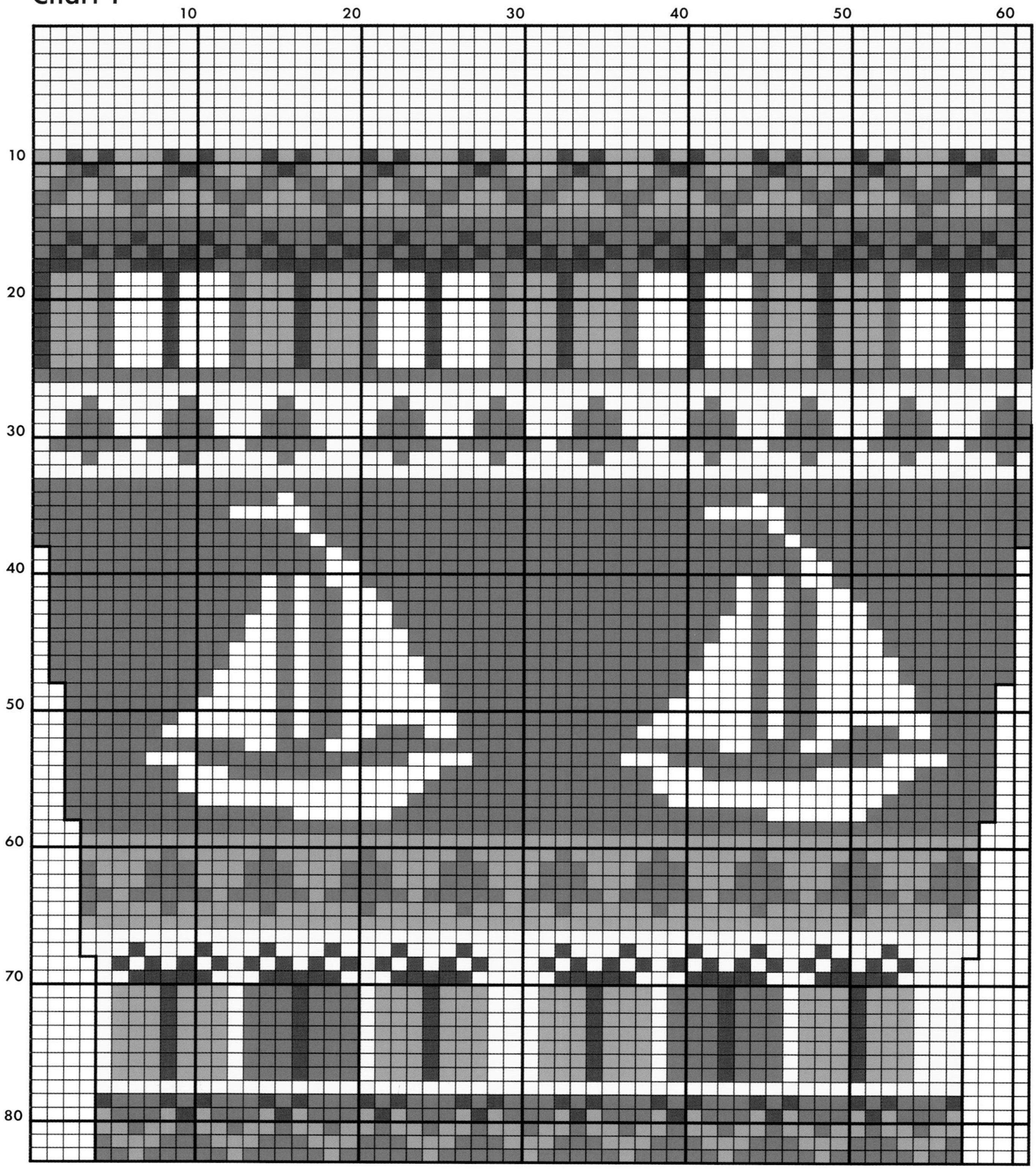

Knitted Christmas Stockings

Chart 2

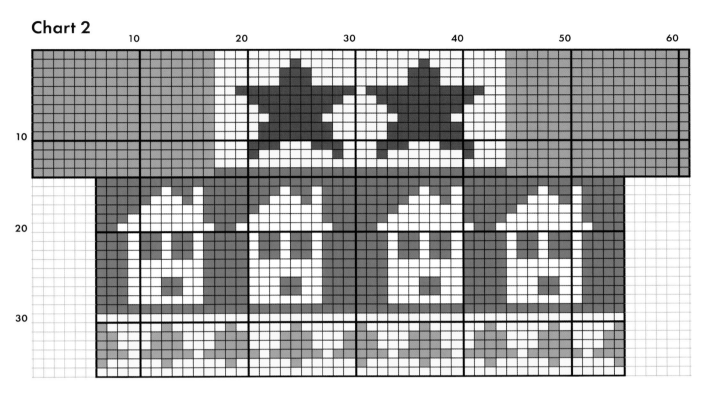

Ice-skating Fun

Skill level

Materials
- Pair of 3.5mm (US4) knitting needles
- 3.5mm (US4) double-pointed knitting needles
- Red Heart Super Saver, 100% acrylic (364yd/333m per 198g ball):
  1 x 198g ball in Cherry Red, Aran, White, Light Sage, Paddy Green
- Oddments of Black, Grey Heather, Coffee
- Tapestry needle
- 2 stitch holders
- Jingle bell (optional)

Finished size
22in (56cm) long and 6in (15cm) wide

Starting the stocking
Cast on 60 sts in Cherry Red.
Cuff
Working in k2, p2 rib, continue for 7 rows. Break yarn, leaving about 10in (25cm) for sewing up.

Personalize your stocking
If you would like a name or date on your stocking, use the alphabet and number chart provided on page 138, and a yarn colour of your choice (shown in Cherry Red).
Row 1: P 1 row in Aran.
Row 2: K 1 row and inc 1 st at end of row (61 sts).
Rows 3–9: Continue to p 1 row and k 1 row in Aran for 7 more rows for a total of 9 rows.

Main design

Row 10: Using st st, follow chart 1 on page 112.

Dec 1 st each side on rows 39, 49, 59 and 69 (53 sts).

Work to end of chart 1, end on a p row. Be sure to cross yarns when changing colours to avoid leaving a hole in the work.

Break yarn, leaving an 18in (46cm) end for sewing up.

With RS facing you, sl first 13 sts onto a stitch holder for right half of heel; sl next 27 sts onto a stitch holder for instep; sl last 13 sts onto a dpn for left half of heel.

Left half of heel

With WS facing you, k and p the following rows in Cherry Red.

First row: P.

Next row: Sl 1, k12.

Repeat these two rows for a total of 8 times (18 rows on heel).

Turn heel as follows:

Row 1: P2, p2tog, p1, turn.
Row 2: Sl 1, k3, turn.
Row 3: P3, p2tog, p1, turn.
Row 4: Sl 1, k4, turn.
Row 5: P4, p2tog, p1, turn.
Row 6: Sl 1, k5, turn.
Row 7: P5, p2tog, p1, turn.
Row 8: Sl 1, k6, turn.
Row 9: P6, p2tog, p1 (8 sts).

Break yarn, place sts on stitch holder or leave on needle.

Right half of heel

With RS facing you, k and p the following rows in Cherry Red.

First row: K.

Next row: Sl 1, p12.

Repeat these two rows for a total of 8 times (18 rows on heel).

Turn heel as follows:

Row 1: K2, SKP, k1, turn.
Row 2: Sl 1, p3, turn.
Row 3: K3, SKP, k1, turn.
Row 4: Sl 1, p4, turn.
Row 5: K4, SKP, k1, turn.
Row 6: Sl 1, p5, turn.
Row 7: K5, SKP, k1, turn.

Row 8: Sl 1, p6, turn.
Row 9: K6, SKP, k1 (8 sts).
Break yarn.

Next: Using Cherry Red, k across 8 sts starting on the outer edge of the RS; pick up and k 9 sts on inner edge of half heel. Follow chart 2 on page 113 and k across 27 sts of instep in stocking design; pick up and k 9 sts in red on inner edge of other half heel; k across 8 sts in Cherry Red (61 sts).

P 1 row in same way as above.

Gusset and instep

Row 1: K14, k2tog, k29, SKP, k14 (59 sts).
Row 2: P.
Row 3: K13, k2tog, k29, SKP, k13 (57 sts).
Row 4: P.
Row 5: K12, k2tog, k29, SKP, k12 (55 sts).
Row 6: P.
Row 7: K11, k2tog, k29, SKP, k11 (53 sts).
Row 8: P.
Row 9: K10, k2tog, k29, SKP, k10 (51 sts).
Row 10: P.
Row 11: K9, k2tog, k29, SKP, k9 (49 sts).
Row 12: P.

Follow chart 2 and k 1 row, p 1 row for 24 rows.

Row 25 (decrease row): Continue to follow chart 2, k23, k2tog, k24 (48 sts).
Row 26: P.

Break yarn, leaving a 14in (36cm) end for sewing up.

Shape toe

Row 1: Using Cherry Red, k9, k2tog, k2, SKP, k18, k2tog, k2, SKP, k9 (44 sts).
Row 2: P.
Row 3: K8, k2tog, k2, SKP, k16, k2tog, k2, SKP, k8 (40 sts).
Row 4: P.
Row 5: K7, k2tog, k2, SKP, k14, k2tog, k2, SKP, k7 (36 sts).
Row 6: P.

Row 7: K6, k2tog, k2, SKP, k12, k2tog, k2, SKP, k6 (32 sts).
Row 8: P.
Row 9: K5, k2tog, k2, SKP, k10, k2tog, k2, SKP, k5 (28 sts).
Row 10: P.
Row 11: K4, k2tog, k2, SKP, k8, k2tog, k2, SKP, k4 (24 sts).
Row 12: P.
Row 13: K3, k2tog, k2, SKP, k6, k2tog, k2, SKP, k3 (20 sts).
Row 14: P.
Row 15: K2, k2tog, k2, SKP, k4, k2tog, k2, SKP, k2 (16 sts).

After last row, with WS facing you, place first 4 sts on a dpn. Sl next 8 sts to a second needle and sl last 4 sts to third needle.

Begin with fourth st, sl 4 sts from first needle, k last 4 sts from third needle to same needle with edges at the centre of needle. Needles should be parallel with one another.

Break yarn, leaving a 14in (36cm) length for weaving the toe.

Weaving the toe

Thread end of yarn into tapestry needle and weave sts together as follows:

Front needle: Pass needle through as if to k and sl st off, pass through second st of front needle as if to p but leave st on needle, draw yarn through.

Back needle: Pass needle through as if to p and sl st off, pass through second st of back needle as if to k but leave st on needle, draw yarn through.

Repeat until all sts are joined.

Fasten off.

Completing the stocking

Use a tapestry needle to sew in all ends securely. Weave in all ends using matching colours. Use a mattress stitch to join the seams. Sew the jingle bell onto the toe. To make a chain, use a dpn and cast on 3 sts. K each row until you have the desired length for your chain. Use a tapestry needle to sew the chain onto the top of the stocking.

Ice-skating Fun charts

Each square on the chart represents one stitch.

Key:

- ■ Cherry Red
- □ White
- ■ Paddy Green
- ■ Grey Heather
- □ Aran
- ■ Light Sage
- ■ Black
- ■ Coffee

Chart 1

Chart 2

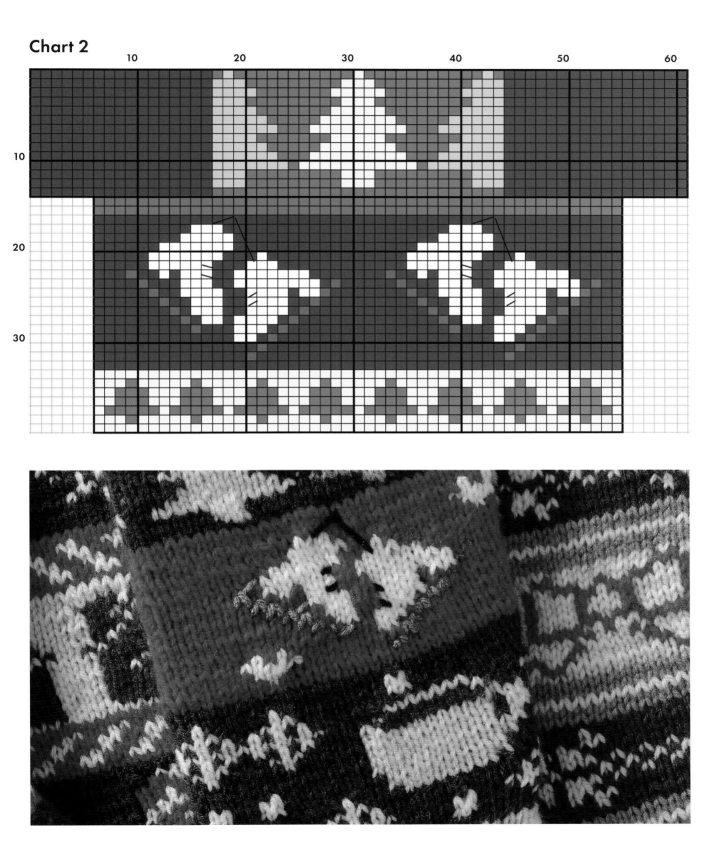

Gingerbread Delight

Skill level
★★★

Materials
- Pair of 3.5mm (US4) knitting needles
- 3.5mm (US4) double-pointed knitting needles
- Red Heart Super Saver, 100% acrylic (364yds/333m per 198g ball):
  1 x 198g ball in Paddy Green, Aran, Cherry Red, White, Coffee
- Tapestry needle
- 2 stitch holders
- Jingle bell (optional)

Finished size
22in (56cm) long and 6in (15cm) wide

Starting the stocking
Cast on 60 sts in Paddy Green.
Cuff
Working in k2, p2 rib, continue for 7 rows. Break yarn, leaving about 10in (25cm) for sewing up.

Personalize your stocking
If you would like a name or date on your stocking, use the alphabet and number chart provided on page 138, and a yarn colour of your choice.
Row 1: P 1 row in Aran.
Row 2: K 1 row and inc 1 st at end of row (61 sts).
Rows 3–9: Continue to p 1 row and k 1 row in Aran for 7 more rows for a total of 9 rows.

Main design

Row 10: Using st st, follow the chart 1 on page 118.

Dec 1 st each side on rows 39, 49, 59 and 69 (53 sts).

Work to end of chart 1, end on a p row. Be sure to cross yarns when changing colours to avoid leaving a hole in the work.

Break yarn, leaving an 18in (46cm) end for sewing up.

With RS facing you, sl first 13 sts onto a stitch holder for right half of heel; sl next 27 sts onto a stitch holder for instep; sl last 13 sts onto a dpn for left half of heel.

Left half of heel

With WS facing you, k and p the following rows in Paddy Green.

First row: P.

Next row: Sl 1, k12.

Repeat these two rows for a total of 8 times (18 rows on heel).

Turn heel as follows:

Row 1: P2, p2tog, p1, turn.
Row 2: Sl 1, k3, turn.
Row 3: P3, p2tog, p1, turn.
Row 4: Sl 1, k4, turn.
Row 5: P4, p2tog, p1, turn.
Row 6: Sl 1, k5, turn.
Row 7: P5, p2tog, p1, turn.
Row 8: Sl 1, k6, turn.
Row 9: P6, p2tog, p1 (8 sts).

Break yarn, place sts on stitch holder or leave on needle.

Right half of heel

With RS facing you, k and p the following rows in Paddy Green.

First row: K.

Next row: Sl 1, p12.

Repeat these two rows for a total of 8 times; 18 rows on heel.

Turn heel as follows:

Row 1: K2, SKP, k1, turn.
Row 2: Sl 1, p3, turn.
Row 3: K3, SKP, k1, turn.
Row 4: Sl 1, p4, turn.
Row 5: K4, SKP, k1, turn.
Row 6: Sl 1, p5, turn.
Row 7: K5, SKP, k1, turn.

Row 8: Sl 1, p6, turn.
Row 9: K6, SKP, k1 (8 sts).
Break yarn.

Next: Using Paddy Green, k across 8 sts starting on the outer edge of the RS; pick up and k 9 sts on inner edge of half heel. Follow chart 2 on page 119 and k across 27 sts of instep in stocking design; pick up and k 9 sts in Paddy Green on inner edge of other half heel; k across 8 sts in Paddy Green (61 sts). P 1 row in same way as above.

Gusset and instep

Row 1: K14, k2tog, k29, SKP, k14 (59 sts).
Row 2: P.
Row 3: K13, k2tog, k29, SKP, k13 (57 sts).
Row 4: P.
Row 5: K12, k2tog, k29, SKP, k12 (55 sts).
Row 6: P.
Row 7: K11, k2tog, k29, SKP, k11 (53 sts).
Row 8: P.
Row 9: K10, k2tog, k29, SKP, k10 (51 sts).
Row 10: P.
Row 11: K9, k2tog, k29, SKP, k9 (49 sts).
Row 12: P.

Follow chart 2 and k 1 row, p 1 row for 22 rows.

Row 23 (decrease row): Continue to follow chart, k23, k2tog, k24 (48 sts).
Row 24: P.

Break yarn, leaving a 14in (36cm) end for sewing up.

Shape toe

Row 1: Using Paddy Green, k9, k2tog, k2, SKP, k18, k2tog, k2, SKP, k9 (44 sts).
Row 2: P.
Row 3: K8, k2tog, k2, SKP, k16, k2tog, k2, SKP, k8 (40 sts).
Row 4: P.
Row 5: K7, k2tog, k2, SKP, k14, k2tog, k2, SKP, k7 (36 sts).
Row 6: P.

Row 7: K6, k2tog, k2, SKP, k12, k2tog, k2, SKP, k6 (32 sts).
Row 8: P.
Row 9: K5, k2tog, k2, SKP, k10, k2tog, k2, SKP, k5 (28 sts).
Row 10: P.
Row 11: K4, k2tog, k2, SKP, k8, k2tog, k2, SKP, k4 (24 sts).
Row 12: P.
Row 13: K3, k2tog, k2, SKP, k6, k2tog, k2, SKP, k3 (20 sts).
Row 14: P.
Row 15: K2, k2tog, k2, SKP, k4, k2tog, k2, SKP, k2 (16 sts).

After last row, with WS facing you, place first 4 sts on a dpn. Sl next 8 sts to a second needle and sl last 4 sts to third needle.

Begin with fourth st, sl 4 sts from first needle, k last 4 sts from third needle to same needle with edges at the centre of needle. Needles should be parallel with one another.

Break yarn, leaving a 14in (36cm) length for weaving the toe.

Weaving the toe

Thread end of yarn into tapestry needle and weave sts together as follows:

Front needle: Pass needle through as if to k and sl st off, pass through second st of front needle as if to p but leave st on needle, draw yarn through.

Back needle: Pass needle through as if to p and sl st off, pass through second st of back needle as if to k but leave st on needle, draw yarn through.

Repeat until all sts are joined.
Fasten off.

Completing the stocking

Use a tapestry needle to sew in all ends securely. Weave in all ends using matching colours. Use a mattress stitch to join the seams. Sew the jingle bell onto the toe. To make a chain, use a dpn and cast on 3 sts. K each row until you have the desired length for your chain. Use a tapestry needle to sew the chain onto the top of the stocking.

Gingerbread Delight charts

Each square on the chart represents one stitch.

Key

- ■ Paddy Green
- ☐ Aran
- ■ Cherry Red
- ☐ White
- ■ Coffee

Chart 1

Knitted Christmas Stockings

Chart 2

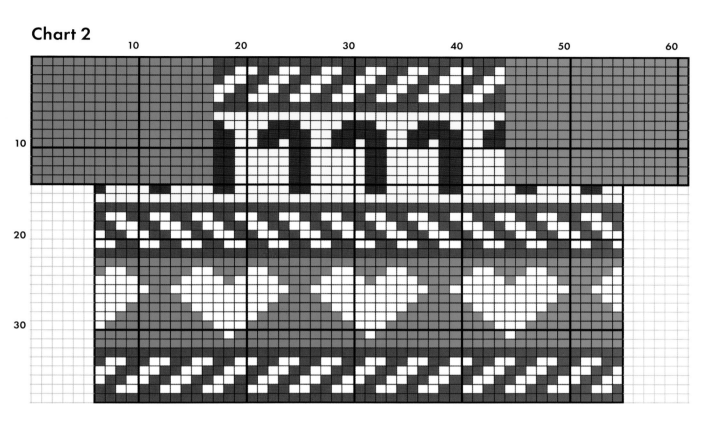

Christmas Bow

Skill level

Materials
- Pair of 3.5mm (US4) knitting needles
- 3.5mm (US4) double-pointed knitting needles
- Red Heart Super Saver, 100% acrylic (364yd/333m per 198g ball): 1 x 198g ball in Paddy Green, Aran, Tea Leaf, Cherry Red
- Tapestry needle
- 2 stitch holders
- Jingle bell (optional)

Finished size
22in (56cm) long and 6in (15cm) wide

Starting the stocking
Cast on 60 sts in Paddy Green.
Cuff
Working in k2, p2 rib, continue for 7 rows. Break yarn, leaving about 10in (25cm) for sewing up.

Personalize your stocking
If you would like a name or date on your stocking, use the alphabet and number chart provided on page 138, and a yarn colour of your choice (shown in Cherry Red).
Row 1: P 1 row in Aran.
Row 2: K 1 row and inc 1 st at end of row (61 sts).
Rows 3–9: Continue to p 1 row and k 1 row in Aran for 7 more rows for a total of 9 rows.

Main design

Row 10: Using st st, follow chart 1 on page 124.

Dec 1 st each side on rows 39, 49, 59 and 69 (53 sts).

Work to end of chart 1, end on a p row.

Be sure to cross yarns when changing colours to avoid leaving a hole in the work.

Break yarn, leaving an 18in (46cm) end for sewing up.

With RS facing you, sl first 13 sts onto a stitch holder for right half of heel; sl next 27 sts onto a stitch holder for instep; sl last 13 sts onto a dpn for left half of heel.

Left half of heel

With WS facing you, k and p the following rows in Paddy Green.

First row: P.

Next row: Sl 1, k12.

Repeat these two rows for a total of 8 times (18 rows on heel).

Turn heel as follows:

Row 1: P2, p2tog, p1, turn.
Row 2: Sl 1, k3, turn.
Row 3: P3, p2tog, p1, turn.
Row 4: Sl 1, k4, turn.
Row 5: P4, p2tog, p1, turn.
Row 6: Sl 1, k5, turn.
Row 7: P5, p2tog, p1, turn.
Row 8: Sl 1, k6, turn.
Row 9: P6, p2tog, p1 (8 sts).

Break yarn, place sts on stitch holder or leave on needle.

Right half of heel

With RS facing you, k and p the following rows in Paddy Green.

First row: K.

Next row: Sl 1, p12.

Repeat these two rows for a total of 8 times (18 rows on heel).

Turn heel as follows:

Row 1: K2, SKP, k1, turn.
Row 2: Sl 1, p3, turn.
Row 3: K3, SKP, k1, turn.
Row 4: Sl 1, p4, turn.
Row 5: K4, SKP, k1, turn.
Row 6: Sl 1, p5, turn.
Row 7: K5, SKP, k1, turn.

Row 8: Sl 1, p6, turn.
Row 9: K6, SKP, k1 (8 sts).
Break yarn.

Next: Using Paddy Green, k across 8 sts starting on the outer edge of the RS; pick up and k 9 sts on inner edge of half heel. Follow chart 2 on page 125 and k across 27 sts of instep in stocking design; pick up and k 9 sts in Paddy Green on inner edge of other half heel; k across 8 sts in Paddy Green (61 sts).

P 1 row in same way as above.

Gusset and instep

Row 1: K14, k2tog, k29, SKP, k14 (59 sts).
Row 2: P.
Row 3: K13, k2tog, k29, SKP, k13 (57 sts).
Row 4: P.
Row 5: K12, k2tog, k29, SKP, k12 (55 sts).
Row 6: P.
Row 7: K11, k2tog, k29, SKP, k11 (53 sts).
Row 8: P.
Row 9: K10, k2tog, k29, SKP, k10 (51 sts).
Row 10: P.
Row 11: K9, k2tog, k29, SKP, k9 (49 sts).
Row 12: P.

Follow chart 2 and k 1 row, p 1 row for 18 rows.

Row 19 (decrease row): Continue to follow chart 2, k23, k2tog, k24 (48 sts).
Row 20: P.

Break yarn, leaving a 14in (36cm) end for sewing up.

Shape toe

Row 1: Using Paddy Green, k9, k2tog, k2, SKP, k18, k2tog, k2, SKP, k9 (44 sts).
Row 2: P.
Row 3: K8, k2tog, k2, SKP, k16, k2tog, k2, SKP, k8 (40 sts).
Row 4: P.
Row 5: K7, k2tog, k2, SKP, k14, k2tog, k2, SKP, k7 (36 sts).
Row 6: P.

Row 7: K6, k2tog, k2, SKP, k12, k2tog, k2, SKP, k6 (32 sts).
Row 8: P.
Row 9: K5, k2tog, k2, SKP, k10, k2tog, k2, SKP, k5 (28 sts).
Row 10: P.
Row 11: K4, k2tog, k2, SKP, k8, k2tog, k2, SKP, k4 (24 sts).
Row 12: P.
Row 13: K3, k2tog, k2, SKP, k6, k2tog, k2, SKP, k3 (20 sts).
Row 14: P.
Row 15: K2, k2tog, k2, SKP, k4, k2tog, k2, SKP, k2 (16 sts).

After last row, with WS facing you, place first 4 sts on a dpn. Sl next 8 sts to a second needle and sl last 4 sts to third needle.

Begin with fourth st, sl 4 sts from first needle, k last 4 sts from third needle to same needle with edges at the centre of needle. Needles should be parallel with one another.

Break yarn, leaving a 14in (36cm) length for weaving the toe.

Weaving the toe

Thread end of yarn into tapestry needle and weave sts together as follows:

Front needle: Pass needle through as if to k and sl st off, pass through second st of front needle as if to p but leave st on needle, draw yarn through.

Back needle: Pass needle through as if to p and sl st off, pass through second st of back needle as if to k but leave st on needle, draw yarn through.

Repeat until all sts are joined.

Fasten off.

Completing the stocking

Use a tapestry needle to sew in all ends securely. Weave in all ends using matching colours. Use a mattress stitch to join the seams. Sew the jingle bell onto the toe. To make a chain, use a dpn and cast on 3 sts. K each row until you have the desired length for your chain. Use a tapestry needle to sew the chain onto the top of the stocking.

Christmas Bow charts

Each square on the chart represents one stitch.

Key:
◼ Paddy Green ◼ Cherry Red
◻ Tea Leaf ◻ Aran

Chart 1

Chart 2

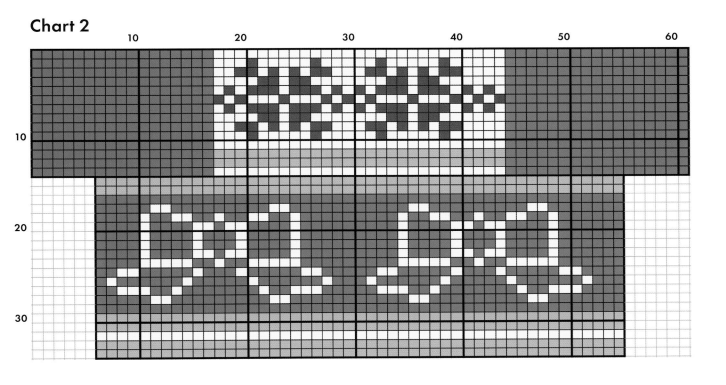

Essential Know-how

Tools and Materials

Before you start to knit, you'll need to gather some essential tools and materials. If you already know how to knit, you may already have most of the tools needed. Each stocking requires a small number of materials to make knitting cost efficient.

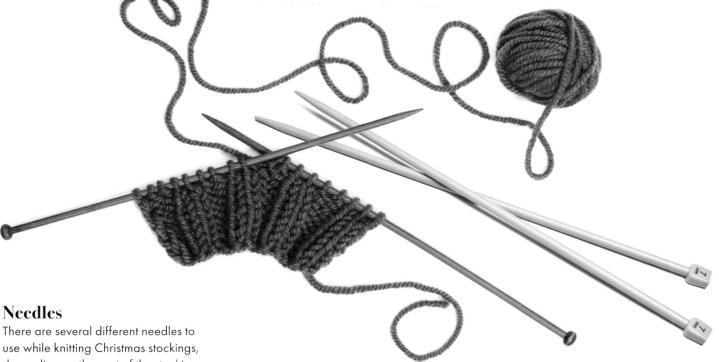

Needles

There are several different needles to use while knitting Christmas stockings, depending on the part of the stocking you are working on.

First, you will need a set of knitting needles, which come in a variety of sizes. The smaller you go, the smaller your stitches will be. Be sure to check the recommended needle size on the ball band. Next, you will need four lightweight, 3.5m (US4) double-pointed needles as well as a good-quality tapestry needle to sew the ends together. A size 5mm crochet hook allows you to weave in all the ends once the stocking is complete, and two stitch holders will hold your work as you begin the left and right half of the heels.

Find knitting needles that are comfortable and make knitting easier. A lightweight aluminium knitting needle can make knitting easier and reduce yarn splitting. Some people recommend bamboo, which is ideal for long hours of knitting. These types of knitting needles reduce strain on your hands because of their smooth texture.

However, it is completely up to you. Be sure to test knitting needles before you make a purchase, and don't be afraid to ask questions and opinions of shop owners.

Yarn

There are a variety of yarn types. The yarn used for most of the Christmas stockings in this book is 100% acrylic aran (worsted) weight. This type of yarn will last for many years. Each yarn ball includes clear instructions to make it easy to know what needle to use. Spend some quality time in a yarn shop. Get to know the yarn, read the labels and ask questions.

Accessories

Accessories are not essential but can be a way to beautify your stocking. To add a fun accessory to your Christmas stockings, here are a few options.

First, sew a jingle bell onto the toe before you close up the stocking. Another idea is to add a tassel using fine or light-type yarn and some 14–16mm wooden beads. Also, you could sew on some sequins.

Knitting Basics

Here you will find information on how to cast on, make basic knitting stitches and patterns, cast off and work with various colours.

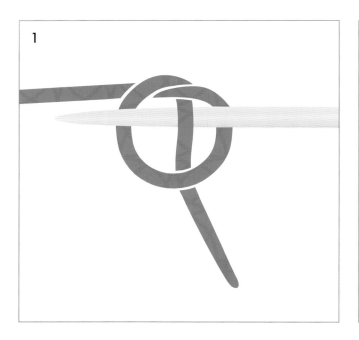

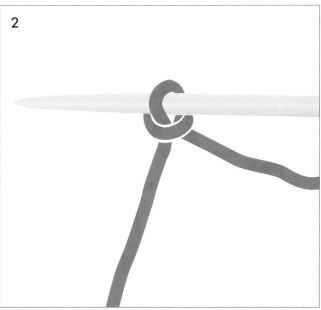

Slip knot

First create a slip knot before casting stitches onto the needle.

1 Take the long end of the yarn attached to the ball, wrap it around your fingers and cross the yarn to form a pretzel shape. Insert the needle under the first loop.

2 Pull the yarn tight to create your first stitch.

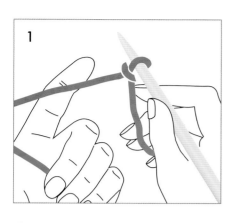

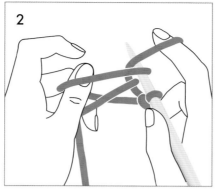

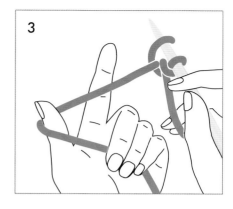

Casting on

1 First, leave about 3ft (90cm) of yarn. Make a slip knot and place on the needle. Pull both ends tight to create one stitch. Hold the needle in your right hand and hold the end of the yarn in your left hand. Loop the yarn around your left thumb.

2 Insert the needle into the loop on your thumb from front to back. Wind the yarn over the point of the needle from back to front.

3 Pass the point of the needle through the loop on your thumb from back to

front, easing the loop off the thumb. Pull the yarn in your left hand to tighten the stitch around the needle. Repeat the steps to create the stitches noted in each pattern. There should be a short tail of about 6in (15cm) long left over to use to sew the two ends together as each stocking is knitted flat.

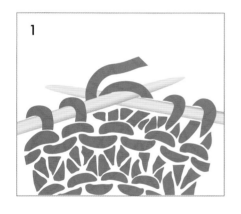

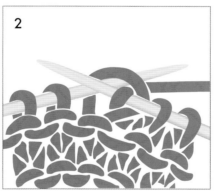

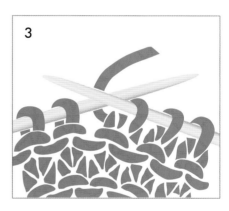

Knit stitch

Now that you have all of your stitches placed on your needle, you are ready to knit. Knitting is basic and once you learn the technique you will be ready to learn a purl stitch. A knit stitch creates a bump that looks like a little 'v'.

1 Hold your needle with the stitches in your left hand and the empty needle and yarn in your right hand. Insert the empty needle through the front of the first cast-on stitch from front to back. Wrap the yarn around the point of the right needle.

2 Draw the wrapped yarn through the first cast-on stitch by bringing the right needle down, under and up in front of the left needle.

3 Slide the stitch off the left needle to create a stitch. Repeat the steps until you knit all the cast-on stitches.

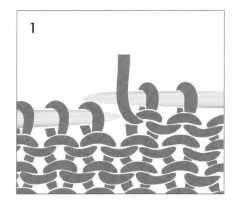

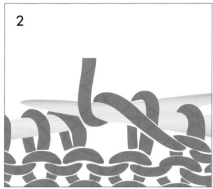

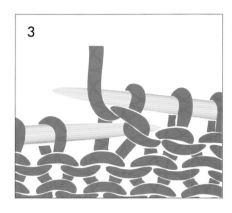

Purl stitch

A purl stitch is slightly different from a knit stitch. Purl stitches have little horizontal 'bumps' in front of them.

1 Hold your needle with the stitches in your left hand and the empty needle and yarn in your right. Insert the empty needle through the front of the first cast-on stitch from back to front. Did you notice that you go back to front instead of front to back? That is the main difference.

2 Wrap the yarn around the point of the right needle. Draw the wrapped yarn through the first cast-on stitch by bringing the right needle down, under and up in the back of the left needle.

3 Slide the stitch off the left needle to create a stitch. Repeat the steps until you purl all the stitches.

Stitch patterns

Garter Stitch

This is a fancy term for knitting every stitch on every row. This stitch isn't used for any of the stockings in the book, but it is important to understand.

Example 1: Stocking Stitch

This basic knitting stitch pattern creates a smooth, even fabric. Made by knitting alternating rows of knit and purl stitches, this pattern is perfect for beginners and is easy to learn. All of the stockings use the stocking stitch pattern. The front side of the fabric looks like a series of Vs (A), while the wrong side resembles bumps (B).

Example 2: Ribbing

Rib stitch is a textured vertical stripe stitch and is created by alternating knit and purl stitches in the same row. Each of the Christmas stockings has a k2, p2 pattern, which means knitting two stitches and then purling two stitches until the end of the row. It creates a beautiful cuff for the stocking. Below are two examples to use, with the second one preferred. A popular option is to personalize a stocking. After creating a cuff of seven rows, you can knit a name.

Example 2A: Single rib

Row 1: *K1, p1; rep from * to the end of the row. Repeat row 1 for ribbing (knit one stitch, purl one stitch, and alternate).

Example 2B: Double rib

Row 1: *K2, p2; rep from * to the end of the row (knit two stitches, purl two stitches, and alt). Rep row 1 for ribbing.

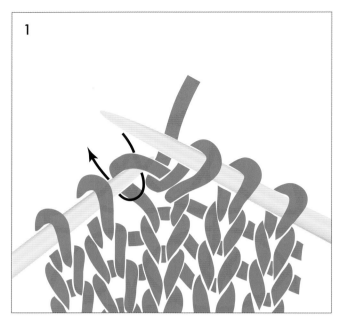

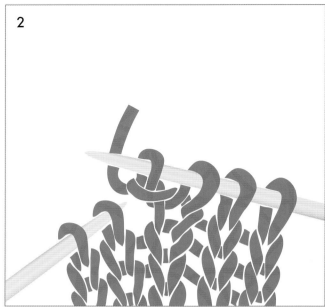

Increasing

An increase in a knitting pattern allows you to add stitches. There are two methods used in the Christmas stocking patterns. Practise the following methods, casting on 20 stitches. Use the stocking stitch for a few rows, ending with a purl row.

Method 1

Knit into the front and back of the same stitch. Use this method when working a right side (knit stitch row).

First knit the first stitch in the usual way, but do not slip it off the needle yet. Insert the right needle into the back of the next stitch from the left needle. Then wrap the yarn around the needle clockwise and slide the needle through.

Method 2

Use the lifted increase method when working a wrong side (purl stitch row).

First insert the right needle from back to front under the horizontal strand of yarn between the stitch just worked and the next stitch. Then wrap the yarn around the needle clockwise and slide the needle through.

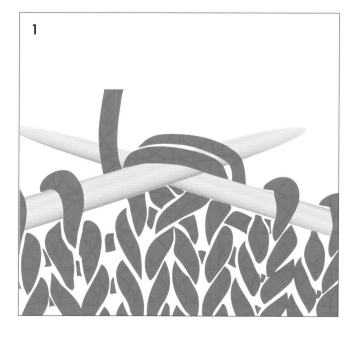

Decreasing

A decrease in a knitting pattern allows you to reduce two or more stitches into one. The easiest decrease in knitting is called k2tog – knit two together. It is simply knitting two stitches instead of one, which creates a right-slanting stitch.

1 First, insert your right knitting needle into the first two stitches on the left needle. Wrap the yarn around the point of the right needle. Then bring the right needle down, under and up to the back of the left needle. Slide the stitches off the left needle to create a stitch.

Another method called SKP (Slip, Knit and Pass) can also be used. First slip the next stitch knitwise off the left needle onto the right needle. Then knit the next stitch. Next, pass the slipped stitch over the knit stitch and off the needle.

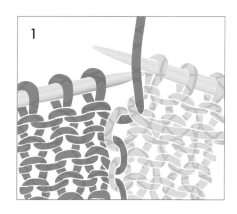

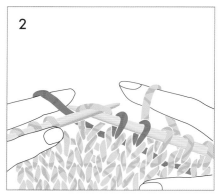

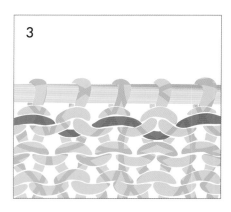

Colour work

Knitting with a variety of colours may seem difficult, but it's actually quite simple. Colour work knitting is the term that covers all types of knitting with a multiple of colours in a single row to create a pattern. Each of the stocking patterns has a variety of colours so this term will be important to understand. There are two types of colour work in knitting, including stranded and intarsia. This book uses the intarsia method, which is used when you have an unlimited number of different colours in a row.

At the point where you need to change colours, simply drop the first colour and pick up the second. Be sure to cross yarns when changing colours to avoid leaving a hole in the work. Each square on the graph represents one stitch. When you knit, read the chart from left to right and when you purl, read the chart right to left.

My grandma taught me to use bobbins to hold each colour but it has been years since I've used them. It is probably a good idea in the beginning so that you have an easier time keeping track of each colour. However, if you have more than five colours in a row, they may get tangled so it is definitely a preferred choice.

Weaving in loose ends

This takes place after completing the toe, when you need to weave in all of the ends to get rid of the loose dangling yarn ends left over.

First, be sure that the stitch isn't super loose on the other side. Next, weave in all ends using matching colours in a few of the stitches. I tend to weave the loose ends in at least three bumps. Be sure to leave a tiny tail.

Picking up stitches

This technique is used after completing the right heel of the stocking. With needle and yarn, knit across eight stitches starting on the outer edge. Next, you will pick up the stitches. Insert the needle under the two slip stitch strands, wrap the yarn around and pull a knit stitch through. Continue until you have 17 stitches on your needle. Next, knit the 27 stitches of the instep. Next, pick up nine stitches and knit across eight stitches.

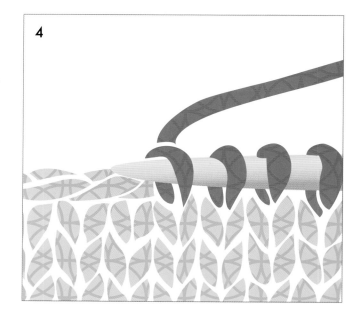

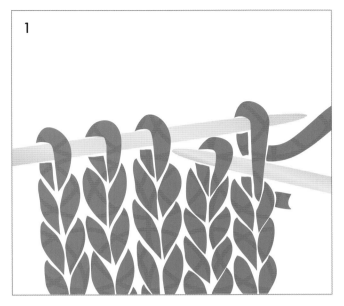

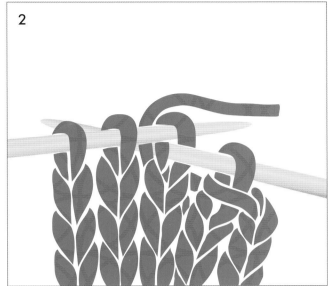

Casting off

This is the final step of your knitting project and very important so that your project doesn't unravel. There are two different ways to cast off; this teaches you how to cast off knitwise and purlwise. You will not need to cast off knitwise or purlwise on these stockings, but it is important to understand this concept as it is in most knitting projects.

Cast off knitwise

1 Knit the first two stitches on your knitting needle.
2 Next, insert your left needle into the first stitch you knit on your right needle. Lift the first stitch over the second stitch and drop it off the needle. You will now only have one stitch on the needle. Knit another stitch and repeat step two until you

have only one stitch left. Finally, with the last stitch on your right needle, cut your yarn and be sure to leave a tail long enough to weave in later. Draw the tail through the remaining stitch and pull it snug.

Cast off purlwise

If you have a knitting pattern that asks you to cast off in purl stitch, this is easy to do. Instead of knitting the stitches, simply purl them. Repeat the process as for casting off knitwise, until you've worked all the stitches.

Mattress stitch

This is a finishing technique that can be used for vertical seaming. It creates an invisible join between pieces worked in a stocking stitch. To do this, use the tail left from the toe or cut a new piece of yarn. Be sure to use matching colours. Thread through a tapestry needle. Insert the needle into the first and second horizontal bar on the right side. Next, insert your needle through the next two bars on the left-hand piece of knitting. Pull the needle and yarn through and repeat on the right side.

Personalize

I love personalizing Christmas stockings. As a child, I enjoyed finding a souvenir with my name on it, but because my name is spelled differently, it was always tricky to find its exact spelling. This solves the issue! After knitting the ribbing, use the alphabet graph below to knit the name (and the date, if you want) onto the stocking.

Here are the instructions:

1 P 1 row in your colour of choice and inc 1 st at the end of the row.

2 Continue to use stocking stitch in the same colour for 7 more rows for a total of 9 rows.

3 If you would like a name or date on your stocking, use the alphabet number chart provided and a contrast colour of choice. Be sure to draw out the name beforehand (on the blank chart opposite) and to follow each square.

4 Once the 9 rows are complete, follow the rest of the colour chart given for the pattern.

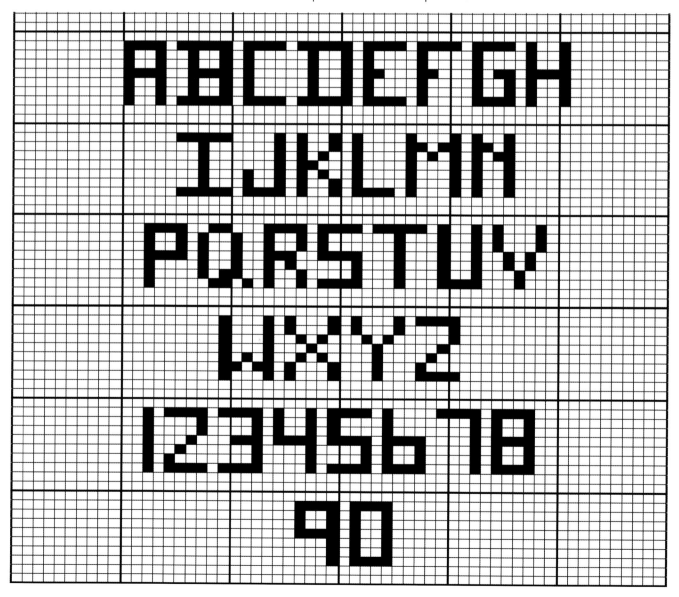

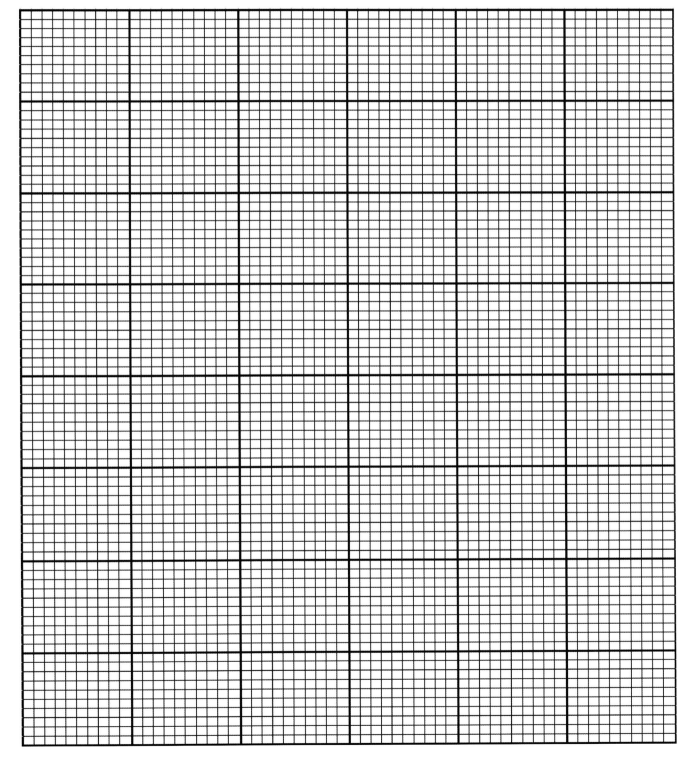

Abbreviations

Co	cast on	**SKP**	slip, knit, pass stitch over – one stitch decreased
Dec	decrease		
Dpn(s)	double-pointed needle(s)	**Sl**	slip
Inc	increase	**St(s)**	stitch(es)
K	knit	**St st**	stocking stitch (p1 row, k1 row)
P	purl	**Tog**	together
RS	right side	**WS**	wrong side

Conversions

Knitting needles

UK	Metric	US
14	2mm	0
13	2.25mm	1
12	2.75mm	2
11	3mm	–
10	3.25mm	3
–	3.5mm	4
9	3.75mm	5
8	4mm	6
7	4.5mm	7
6	5mm	8
5	5.5mm	9
4	6mm	10
3	6.5mm	10.5
2	7mm	10.5
1	7.5mm	11
0	8mm	13
000	10mm	15

Yarn weight

UK	US
Double knitting	Light worsted
Aran	Worsted

UK/US terms

UK	US
Cast off	Bind off
Stocking stitch	Stockinette stitch
Tension	Gauge
Yarn round needle	Yarn over

I dedicate this book to my Grandma Grant
and my sweet angel Elizabeth.

First published 2023 by
Guild of Master Craftsman Publications Ltd
Castle Place, 166 High Street, Lewes,
East Sussex BN7 1XU

Text © Emilee Reynolds, 2023
Copyright in the Work © GMC Publications Ltd, 2023

ISBN 978-1-78494-668-5

All rights reserved

The right of Emilee Reynolds to be identified as the author of this work has
been asserted in accordance with the Copyright, Designs and Patents Act
1988, sections 77 and 78.

No part of this publication may be reproduced, stored in a retrieval system
or transmitted in any form or by any means without the prior permission of
the publisher and copyright owner.

This book is sold subject to the condition that all designs are copyright and
are not for commercial reproduction without the permission of the designer
and copyright owner.

While every effort has been made to obtain permission from the copyright
holders for all material used in this book, the publishers will be pleased to
hear from anyone who has not been appropriately acknowledged and to
make the correction in future reprints.

The publishers and author can accept no legal responsibility for any
consequences arising from the application of information, advice or
instructions given in this publication.

A catalogue record for this book is available from the British Library.

Publisher Jonathan Bailey
Production Jim Bulley
Senior Project Editor Susie Behar
Pattern Checker Jude Roust
Design Manager Robin Shields
Designer Cathy Challinor
Photographer Andrew Perris
Stylist Anna Stevens

Colour origination by GMC Reprographics
Printed and bound in China

Acknowledgements

It has been a dream of mine to produce a Christmas stocking knitting book. Special thanks to Paul Eckersley, Jonathan Bailey, Charlotte Mockridge, Virginia Brehaut, Jude Roust, Susie Behar and anyone else at GMC Publications who helped with this book.

Thank you to Adrienne Chandler from Let's Knit magazine for featuring my Forest Friends Collection and to Amanda Robinson from Simply Knitting magazine for featuring my A Colorful World Collection. I'm grateful for the opportunities.

Finally thank you so much to my family and friends, especially my husband, Adrian who has encouraged me to add more beads. He is truly the greatest editor of my designs. Thank you to my children, Eli, Elizabeth, and Olivia, I love you all. Thanks to my grandma, Carol Grant who taught me how to knit and for giving me the opportunity to continue the family tradition. And thanks to my parents who have always supported and believed in me. I really do appreciate ALL of you. Keep on dreaming!

About the author

Taught to knit by her grandmother, Emilee Reynolds has been creating unique stockings for family and clients ever since. She began her blog, Sweetly Made (just for you), to share her passion for knitting. She sells patterns and stockings through her successful Etsy shop and Ravelry. Emilee's work has been featured in *Let's Knit* and *Simply Knitting* magazines. She lives in Mesa, Arizona, with her family.

To order a book, contact:

GMC Publications Ltd
Castle Place, 166 High Street,
Lewes, East Sussex,
BN7 1XU
United Kingdom
Tel: +44 (0)1273 488005
www.gmcbooks.com